STAGE FIGHTS

STAGE FIGHTS

A simple handbook of techniques

by

GILBERT GORDON
A.T.D., L.R.A.M., L.G.S.M., A.D.B.

Adviser Speech and Drama, Northamptonshire
Examiner for the English Speaking Board
Examiner for the Guildhall School of Music and Drama
Member of the Guild of Drama Adjudicators
Member of the Society of Teachers of Speech and Drama
Bronze, Silver and Gold Medal, Amateur Fencing Association

Drawings by the Author

Foreword by

MAISIE COBBY

NEW YORK
THEATRE ARTS BOOKS

FIRST PUBLISHED IN THE
UNITED STATES IN 1973 BY
THEATRE ARTS BOOKS
333 SIXTH AVENUE
NEW YORK 10014

ISBN 0 - 87830 - 131 - 3

Library of Congress Catalog No. 73 - 75918

To

MAISIE

for the help and encouragement
that made this book possible

PRINTED IN GREAT BRITAIN BY
THE BOWERING PRESS
PLYMOUTH

FOREWORD

ALL who are concerned with the Theatre Arts, whether as actors, producers, technicians, or as teachers and lecturers in the field of Education, will find in this Handbook a wealth of stimulating information and instruction on the art of fencing and all types of sword play for stage purposes.

The book is written with special emphasis on the work now being done in our schools, youth clubs and art centres, where all aspects of Drama and the Allied Arts have a legitimate place and are closely integrated within the total curriculum.

The author covers both the artistic and technical sides of the subject, and every process is carefully and lucidly explained and illustrated with a profusion of photographs and drawings. An added interest is the selection of literary and dramatic passages in which fights occur, such as the opening of *Romeo and Juliet*, the battle scene from *Julius Caesar*, the duel scenes from *Hamlet* and *Cyrano de Bergerac*, and the Robin Hood plays and pageants. These and many others are illustrated in detail to help the teacher in his classroom work. Further, there are hints on the making of essential weapons and the appropriate costume for each occasion.

The author is a recognised authority in this art, and has been a County Team fencer in three counties; his favourite weapon is the Épée. He has currently done a great deal of coaching with the A.F.A. Bronze, Silver and Gold Standard Scheme and uses fencing techniques as part of his many training courses. He has had wide and varied experience in lecturing, producing and performing, both in the professional theatre and in education.

As one who has seen Mr. Gordon in action and has a high regard for his work, I consider that this publication will prove of outstanding value, and one from which both teachers and students will reap rich rewards.

MAISIE COBBY

CONTENTS

ILLUSTRATIONS

There were many schools of Fencing, and some of the more famous masters wrote books and had their favourite attacks and guards illustrated, in some cases by famous artists. The drawings and sketches are based on illustrations in books by the masters—FABRIS, CAPO FERRO, LABAT and DANET, amongst others.

CREDITS

The author wishes to thank the following for their help:—

Chappell and Co.. Fig. 7;

Brian J. Douglas, F.R.P.S., Fig. 10;

Norfolk News Co. Ltd., Norwich, jacket photo;

Northamptonshire Newspapers Ltd., Kettering, Fig. 4;

Studio John Norman, King's Lynn, Fig. 18;

Mr. Ken Parry, Physical Education Adviser,
Northamptonshire;

Mr. Dennis Conie, Visual Aid Adviser,
Northamptonshire, Figs. 3, 5, 6, 9, 11, 14 and 20;

The Beanfield Secondary School, Corby,
Northamptonshire, Figs, 25, 26, 27;

Boot and Shoe College, Rushden, Northamptonshire,
Figs. 23 and 24;

Croyland Road Junior School, Northampton, Fig. 1;

Roade Secondary School, Northamptonshire, Figs.
23, 25;

Moulton Secondary School, Northamptonshire, Figs.
27, 29;

Weavers Comprehensive School, Wellingborough,
Fig. 30.

INTRODUCTION

AFTER many years of teaching stage fight techniques to small boys and girls in junior schools to enable them to give convincing performances as Robin Hood, the Turkish Knight, or St. George; coaching athletic teenagers how to approach the "rumble" in *West Side Story*, or improvise a group combat, and occasionally helping Women's Institutes and Townswomen's Guild ladies to put over a passable display of swording, I am convinced that a simple handbook such as this will open up an exciting new world of active plays to a wide variety of people, and be of value to teachers and youth leaders, faced with the difficult task of putting on a stage fight or combat, convincingly and with maximum safety.

The skill and naturalism with which the best professional theatres mount these spectacles, combining direction and choreography, makes it imperative that more time and care is devoted to the art by the amateur theatre, especially as the combat is usually a dramatic climax in the play. Excellent work in improvisation, and dance drama is being done today in schools and youth clubs and it is a short step from a confrontation with a partner, to a safe and excitingly dramatic stage fight.

There is the point too that an actor, taking part in a stage fight, must do so in character. This is particularly true in a play like *Romeo and Juliet*, and Shakespeare has made it easy by describing how Mercutio and Tybalt, and subsequently Romeo, confront each other. A study of the fight will help the actor to develop and build a rounded character. It is not intended to formulate a set of rules but the suggestions and illustrations may stimulate imagination and encourage experiment.

1

As travelling companies have shown, boys and girls will become fighting armies at the drop of a hat, and revel in the experience—miming hewing and hacking with the greatest enthusiasm—dying unwillingly when necessary on the strict understanding that they are resurrected fairly promptly. In the playground they will slap at each

Fig. 1

Fig. 1. Children from Croyland Road Junior School, Wellingborough, using movable stage equipment to storm a castle.

other with sticks in a most dangerous manner, and girls these days take a very active part in these activities and incidentally make excellent fencers.

All this is a natural part of growing up; it is bound up with self-assertion, pride, ambition and the desire to be an individual. But children's fights are fights of peace, they do not seek to kill or maim or obliterate, and in general they are healthy.

Anyone who has taken part in a fencing match, will understand the exhilaration of mind and body stimulated by the "playing chess at lightning speed" and the satisfaction of outwitting an opponent. They will also know the importance of courtesy and friendly disciplined behaviour.

Safety Precautions

Particularly in the early stages of stage fight sequences, I cannot too strongly emphasise the necessity for safety precautions and personally I always insist that the combatants wear fencing masks and épée jackets until such time as they have the sequences firmly in their minds and are unlikely to "dry up" during the exercise. When the passage is firmly fixed in the minds of both, the jackets and helmets can be dispensed with but, even then, the precaution of stopping the blow or making a thrust short should be firmly kept in mind; and a sense of distance is imperative. Personally too I try to avoid involving nervous or over-belligerent personnel in bouts and, if the actor is not fully co-ordinated and controlled, he would be better left out for his own safety and that of others.

I think stage fighting is of the department of drama, not of sport, and is primarily acting with weapons. Every move must be carefully arranged beforehand or there can be no safety in the exercise. Free play in a fencing club can often be chaotic but this must never be allowed to happen in a stage fight. The fight director's job is to choreograph the entire event in the same way as a dance or ballet and, if it helps memory, a fight should be written down. Consideration should certainly be given to the amount of space available and what scenery and properties are on during the scene. The actors must be rehearsed diligently day after day, if possible, until they are as near perfect as they can possibly be.

Obviously the fight director must be in continuous

conference with the stage director regarding starting and finishing positions and, above all, fights must be in character and fit into the producer's conception of the overall play.

Fencers aim to hit, actors to miss their target, and whereas good fencers often fight at a speed and with technical dexterity that bemuses the layman, the actor, though he may sometimes have to fight quickly, must think in every instance of the audience and ensure that they see what is happening.

It is a good idea to use a musical background, particularly during period fencing. This may emphasise the action and would certainly help the timing of the participants.

The business of stage fighting calls for concentration and diligence and particularly trust in one's opponent. It is certainly no activity for the ego-maniac. Safety must be the first consideration at all times and sequence arrangements must be carefully and meticulously adhered to.

The idea of the book then is to give a series of safe but exciting formulas for a wide variety of stage fights which will allow the maximum dramatic excitement with the minimum danger to children, and to give clear ideas of fight situations which any teacher or youth leader can use.

Words are poor material to describe action, but the many photographs will help towards a clearer picture.

CHAPTER I

BACKGROUND

THE weapon is the symbol of the commitment of man to the greatest good. He who is unwilling to defend himself against what he recognises as evil, discards all that makes life worthwhile, and surrenders himself and not himself alone. Memorable plays are concerned with life and death, and nothing expresses the involvement of life with death as does the age-old weapons of man. The weapon secured his food, preserved his life, and accompanied him in death.

The weapon stood for freedom, strength and manhood. Strength ranks next to wisdom and is tempered by moderation. Justice is a sword to control abuse of power and remove injustice from the world. The fashioned weapon was never a crude means of destruction, it had a symbolic value as something lofty and artistic. There are stone age daggers of unsurpassed artistic achievement showing a desire for harmony, self-expression, permanence and perfection.

The medieval king went into battle in the greatest panoply. His life-risking challenge was a pageant with the threat of death. Jousting, shooting and hunting were also solemn occasions; engineering and technical skill made sure the weapon was reliable, but the art of the goldsmith and silversmith was also important to impress the ladies. The weapon was also a badge of rank and a man did not carry one above his station. The Emperor Maximilian I had his triumphal procession painted on parchment to depict the social order, and this order was shown by the weapons carried by the various ranks. Chaucer's Miller in *The Reeves Tale* carried—a sword, a cutlass (round his neck), a "Popper", a poniard, and a big knife—a nice selection of cutlery.

When the handling of weapons was part of a man's education, like riding and dancing and etiquette, theatre audiences must have been extremely critical, and it is worth note that two members of the company at Shakespeare's *Globe* were fencing masters: one was Tarlton the comic and the other Christopher Sly, who created the part of Romeo. Ben Jonson, too, killed a man in a duel and was branded on the thumb.

Peg Woffington brought the famous Angelo from Dublin and he founded a fencing and riding school under royal patronage; no doubt when she played her breeches parts at Garrick's Theatre, she took part in stage fighting with his help and instruction, in addition to displaying her handsome calves.

The great Victorian actors, Irving, Bancroft, Tree, Terry and others were all fencers; and, with the help of Felix Bertrand the Master of Fence, memorable fights were mounted and these were popular with the audience and saved many a poor play. Present-day lightweight armour of fibreglass speeds up the action, but on one occasion I wore a real suit of armour and found I could move in comfort after a little practice. I am sure the visual movement and the actual fight gained a great deal from the "real thing" and one could cut away at the opponent's body and limbs in safety, widening the scope of the fight considerably.

Imaginative and talented fight arrangers are at work in our theatres today, and film and television fights are also of a high standard. The names of Professor Bob Anderson, William Hobbs, and John Barton, and many others spring to mind. Often too little account is taken of the talent displayed by these gentlemen. On the other hand a Society of Fight Directors has just been founded, and this body may revolutionize the situation. An opportunity to discuss methods and ideas would help all Masters.

CHAPTER II

FENCING

Theory

F OR those interested in fencing, an explanation of some of the terms used may be of interest.

The *Foil* is the basic weapon. Its principal features are shown in the diagram:

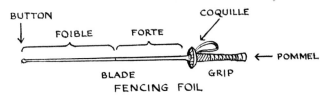

Fig. 2

Blade Guard to Point (Button)—35 $\frac{3}{8}$ *inches.*

Diameter of Guard—less than 4 $\frac{3}{4}$ *inches.*

Weight—less than 17 $\frac{5}{8}$ ounces.

Length (inside Guard to Pommel)—9 $\frac{1}{2}$ inches.

The *On Guard* position with bent knees, enabling a fencer to move easily backwards and forwards and to defend himself and to attack, is known as the *Basic Position* (see Fig. 3, pp. 10 and 11).

The *Parry* (beating off an attack) is designed to protect the four divisions of the target: high right, low right, high left and low left. There are eight positions of the sword hand corresponding to the parries and the *lines of engagement* (where the hand is in *supination*, the fingers are pointing upwards; in *pronation*, the fingers are pointing downwards). The Parries are:

1. Prime	low left	pronation
2. Seconde	low right	pronation
3. Tierce	high right	pronation
4. Quarte	high left	supination
5. Quinte (low Quarte)	low left	pronation
6. Sixte	high right	supination
7. Septime	low left	supination
8. Octave	low right	supination

The Quarte and Sixte are the most useful. Next in importance are the Septime and Octave (see Figs, 3, 14, 16 and 17, pp. 10–11, 84–86, 90–92).

The *Development* covers the *Extension* of the sword arm (indicating the attacker) followed by the *Lunge*. Returning to the On Guard position is called the *Recovery*. *Fencing Measure* means the distance in which a fencer can hit his opponent with a full lunge, and his opponent must lunge to hit him. Take note that in stage fencing the opponents are always out of measure, and do not aim to hit each other.

Temps d'Escrime (*Fencing Time*) indicates the time taken by a fencer to execute a movement of blade, arm, body or legs, or any of these simultaneously.

There are two main groups of *Offensive*.

1. Simple Attacks: Direct by straight thrust; Indirect by disengage (see Fig. 12, p. 75), cut-over or counter disengage.

2. Compound Attacks which include one or more feints.

The principle of *Defence* is to *Oppose* the forte (the thick part of the blade to the foible (the thinner part towards the point) in deflecting the attacking weapon.

There are three types of parry:

1. Simple, which is an instinctive direct parry.
2. Semi-circular, which is indirect and low (see Fig. 17).
3. Circular, which is counter and acquired (see Fig. 16, p. 90).

All parries can be executed by opposition or detachment

and successive parries are a combination of two or more of these.

Offensive action following a successful parry is known as a *Riposte* and offensive action, following a successful parry of a riposte, is called a *Counter Riposte*, Counter ripostes are numbered, the attacker making the odd-numbered counter ripostes and the defender making the even-numbered ones. Ripostes can be simple or compound and may be executed at once or after a delay.

A *Stop Hit* is a counter attack made on an opponent's attack, but to be successful it must arrive before the attack. A hit on a step forward, on a preparation, or on an opponent who attacks with a bent arm would be successful. A stop hit which is covered is called a *Time Hit* (see Fig. 20, p. 98).

Contre Temps (*Counter Time*) indicates that a fencer has drawn a stop hit or a time hit from his opponent, and has parried and riposted from this *Second Intention*.

If an attack is unsuccessful, it may be renewed by various methods. An immediate replacing of the point after being parried, in the same line without an additional movement of the blade, arm or body, is known as a *Remise*; it is a stop hit on a riposte. A *Redoublement* means a replacing of the point after being parried in the same line or in a different line, by adding a movement of the blade, arm or body. It can be simple or compound. A *Reprise* is a renewal of the attack after returning to the On Guard position, either backward or forward.

Attacks on the Blade

These are made by *a Beat*, which is a crisp movement made against an opponent's blade, with the idea of knocking it aside, or obtaining a reaction. By opening and closing the last fingers, the fencer detaches his sword from his adversary's and brings it back crisply into contact thus knocking it aside.

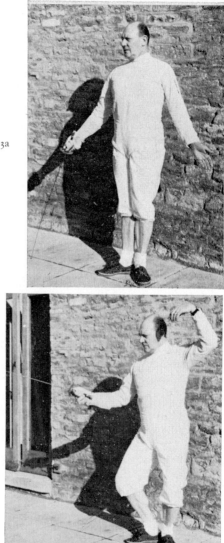

Fig. 3a

Fig. 3b

Fig. 3. Fencing Positions.

(a) Stand upright, feet at right angles, fingers of sword hand pointing upwards (supination), left palm outwards.

(b) Bend the knees forward and outward, bring the sword arm up, keeping
the elbow a handsbreadth from the body. Raise the left arm in a graceful
curve, the left hand relaxed and about six inches above the head.

(c) *On Guard*. Step forward with the right foot, keeping the heels in line, the distance about twice your own foot length. Sit comfortably balanced in the centre of your bent legs.

(d) *Lunge*. Extend the sword arm, keeping your fingers pointing up. Step forward on to your right heel, keeping the right knee above your heel. The left leg becomes straight, and the left arm swings down to balance. The left foot must not roll over but remain flat. To recover, ease off at the left knee, step back with the right foot, swinging the left arm up. Lastly draw back the sword arm to the on guard position.

By *Pressure*, which is an action of pressing upon an opponent's blade to deflect it, or to obtain a reaction. The blades being engaged, the last fingers are contracted, and the wrist flexed, thus exerting a pressure on the blade of the opponent. The movement should be lateral and the blade exerting pressure should not be allowed to drop.

The Froissement can also be used and this is a movement of grazing the opponent's sword strongly and sharply, by bringing the thick part of one's own blade diagonally down from the thin part to the middle of the opposing blade and deflecting it. Tighten the last fingers and flex the wrist into pronation.

Takings of the Blade

When the fencer on guard crosses swords with his opponent he is said to be in a state of *Engagement*, and generally taking the blade is executed against one who has a straight arm with his point threatening the target. Any movement, which deflects the blade while keeping contact with it, is called a taking of the blade.

The Envelopment is an action of taking the thin part of the opponent's sword in the thick part of one's own, and by describing a circle with both blades in contact, returning to the line of engagement. When engaged in sixte (6) rotate the wrist and make the blade describe a circle and the opponent's engaged blade will be carried round and back to the original line of engagement.

The Bind is an action of carrying the opponent's blade diagonally across from a high line to a low line or vice versa, when the swords are engaged. Engaged in sixte, pivot the blade over the opponent's foible (thin part) without moving the arm. Then by opposition of thick to thin parts of the blade, carry the opposing sword from sixte down to septime (on the opposite side) by moving the forearm and flexing the wrist.

The engagement and the change of engagement are

also takings of the blade, and you can prepare for an attack by stepping backwards and forwards. The opponent's blade can be evaded too, or his attempt to beat or take your blade by deception (*The Trompement*), which is a blade action which deceives an opponent's parry. All attacks with the exception of the straight thrust are attacks by trompement, such as indirect and compound attacks. The action of evasion is called *The Derobement*. It is the evading action against an attempt to take or attack the blade.

Remember a taking of the blade can only be successful against an attacker with a straight arm and his point threatening the target. The defender attempts an attack on the blade and this is evaded, then the original attacker has performed a derobement and still has the right of way.

Knowledge of these interesting devices can be helpful, but the ability to make it "Look Right" is much more important to the actor in a stage fight.

Basic Exercises

These are aimed at loosening up the students and introducing them to basic fencing movements: the advance, retire and the development. They are also helpful in introducing the class to the type of concentration needed for stage fighting.

1. Loosen up the students by making them move round to a cheerful piece of music.

2. Relaxing Movement. Investigate balancing points on the body. Slowly bring them up and shake fingers, hands, elbows, shoulders, feet, legs and spine. Divide the group into two teams, each member choosing a partner, and, using a football rattle, make them approach each other in a spiking form of movement. Retreat and then approach each other menacingly. Continue this, exploring in methods of approach, then turn the entire group facing the front and make them stand upright with their feet

Fig. 4. A recreational Fencing Class at the Kettering Youth Centre.

at right-angles; then bend the knees as far as possible outwards and sideways and advance the right foot (or left
foot if left-handed) an easy distance forward so that they
are balanced centrally. Then, keeping the feet near the
ground, step forward with both feet keeping the knees
bent: "advance" (avoid jumping). By the same method
step back and "retire".

3. Now work on concentration, the group advancing
and retiring on the advance or retire of the leader. Divide
into two teams again and advance and retire towards each
other. Turn the entire group forward once more and take
up the bent knee position. Now raise the right (or left)
arm, the elbow a hand's breadth from the body, and shoot
the arm forward and back from the shoulder. Then bring
up the left arm (or right) until the hand is about 6 inches
above the head, the arm making a graceful curve into the
fencing "on guard" position.

4. Shoot forward the right arm, swing down the left
arm for balance, keeping the palm of the hand outwards,
and step forward into a lunge. Now recover to the "on
guard" position and advance, retire and lunge, correcting
faults.

(At this point it is a good plan to use the ordinary
fencing foils and helmets if these are obtainable. However, the mock swords will do equally well, but it is
necessary that the blades should be steel to get the correct feel and sound.)

5. Divide the group into two teams, each member
working with a partner. Make them advance and retire to
each other and cross swords. Call one line A and the other
line B and ensure that they attack alternately. Line A will
now beat lightly on the blades of their opponents who
will maintain a static position, pointing their blades
roughly at their opponents' eye. The beat should be
carried out using pressure of the thumb and forefinger.
Alternate and then counterbeat, e.g. carry the blade under

your opponent's weapon and beat backwards, so that you beat forwards and counterbeat by disengaging and beating back. Now, again using pressure of the thumb and fore-finger, press on the opponent's blade so that you get pressure and ease, pressure and ease alternating. Row A will make a direct attack by straightening the arm and this will be pushed lightly aside by Row B. Alternate, and then Row A will attack directly with a lunge—alternate. Finally, Row A will disengage and attack on both sides, one and two, alternate. Turn the group to the front, feet at right-angles, raise the sword above the head, bring it to the mouth and down to the right in salute, and disperse.

Theory of Striking on Invitation

In the teaching of fencing with all weapons, foil, épée, and sabre, the master creates an opening or invites a point or cut by exposing some part of the body target. The hand and wrist for instance, is opened to receive the thrust or the remise, and the body target cleared to enable the riposte to get home. In exhibitions, too, the situation is "set up" and the fencers learn a sequence of movements. In an ordinary combat the defender has to anticipate where the attack will arrive, and either parry or avoid the point or cut.

In a stage fight where the safety factor is of first im-portance, all point attacks should be made out of distance, so that opponents do *not* hit each other. The final killing thrust is slapped on to the flank, on the blind side of the audience, so that the sword can apparently be run through the actor without the point actually touching him.

When a cutting weapon is used, however, I have found that a suitable formula is the method of attack on invita-tion. Instead of exposing the target as in a fencing exhibi-tion, the defender places his weapon in position and invites an attack on the sword. Great care must be taken by the attacker not to pull the sword, or speed up beyond the safety angle. If the attack is to be made at the head, the attacker will wait until the defender has his weapon in position to defend his head. Careful timing and a little aggressive skirmishing, and possibly a shout on the attack, will carry off this device and the audience will be unaware of the situation. The fighters will have added confidence knowing that they are safe and covered.

In a sabre fight, each defender in turn invites attacks in quinte, sixte and quarte, and the attacker straightening his arm lightly attacks in each quarter. This play will be acceptable if defender and attacker move round each other as if waiting for an opening, then make sudden attacks changing the cadence. Sometimes with a shout and alternating the attack from one side to the other, quite an acceptable amount of drama and excitement is created. The attacks and parries should be bigger and wider than in modern fencing, and the weapon defending should be pushed well away from the body to give the maximum defence.

The Head Parry

The sword is lifted above the head and held parallel to the ground, the hand will have the fingernails pointing down and the back of the hand to the opponent.

Shoulder Parry Right and Left

The sword is held up almost vertical with the point upwards. The hand about six inches below the shoulder, thumb pointing upwards. Carry the forearm right and then across the body to left, braking the wrist.

Right and Left Flank Parry

To parry right or left flank the point of the blade should be lowered. The elbow is kept bent and about a hand's breadth from the body. The right flank parry is a very strong one and similar to Seconde in fencing. The nails are turned down and the back of the hand is uppermost. Turn the hand upwards again for the left flank parry, carry the hand across the body to the inside line. The parry is similar to fencing Septime and not Prime.

Circular Parries

With the rapier and small sword, circular parries may be used to add variety. On the disengage (detaching his blade from yours and bringing it up underneath on the other side and "changing the line") follow his blade round and bring him back to the original line. The circular parry can be made clockwise or anticlockwise.

Parries then can be Simple (instinctive and direct);

Semi-circular (indirect—low)

Circular (counter-acquired)

(See Figs. 16 and 17, pp. 90 and 91.)

Practice of Stance and Group Movement

All aggressive movement should look convincing. It must begin with a semi-crouching position. This is equally true of a wordy battle. Nothing looks worse than an actor leaning from the hips towards his opponent with straight legs. If the knees are slightly bent as one approaches this is more effective dramatically. A position something like the "on guard" position in fencing is a good idea. Thinking in terms of group work, make the class face the instructor, standing with their feet at right-angles (presuming all are right-handed); the right foot will then be pointing towards the leader and the left at right-angles. Then make the class bend the knees as far as possible and take a step forward with the right foot; the distance between the feet should be about twenty-four inches for an average height. Then make them move forward and backward. This can be broken down into stepping forward

weapon, so that it can come forward to the target fairly gently. This is particularly necessary when using heavy weapons, such as the two-handed sword. The whole weight of the body must be put into the effort, particularly the back swing.

The defence positions with the sabre in 1888 are given as Prime, defending a head cut, Tierce and Seconde, covering the outside flank, and Quarte, covering the inside flank. But the master Marozzo, 1536, names nine fencing attacks: Right and left neck, cutting downwards or inwards; right and left of waist and cuts to both kneecaps or the sinews at the back of the knee. The lunge of 1610 and later was wider than the present one with the body thrown forward. For stage purposes the more flamboyant the fencing the better; and the actual attack needs to be worked up by the opponents beating each other's blade, using pressure, and beat and counter-beat, while skirmishing round before an actual attack is launched. Moves like the Bind and the Envelopment also look good and so do broad parries like Prime and Seconde.

The attacker can lift his opponent's blade up and over on either side, thus taking control. The Envelopment is carried out by taking the opposite blade with the thick part of the sword near the hilt, and carrying it round in either a clockwise or anti-clockwise direction. The Bind is similar: dominate the opposing blade and carry the hand with fingers upward, across the body; then reverse the hand, fingers down, and thrust.

Cuts should always be made lightly and be controlled, and may be made at the head, the right and left shoulder and the right and left flank. The method is to straighten the arm towards the target, keeping the point above the opponent's head for a head cut, and by a relaxed movement of the wrist cut downward striking the inviting sword. Turn the hand sideways, thumb to the left, to cut inwards to the opponent's right shoulder, and reverse, thumb to your right, to cut at the left shoulder, each time attacking with the "cutting edge" of your weapon. To attack the flanks, semi-circular cuts downwards and inwards are necessary (see Fig. 11, pp. 71–73).

The Thrust. To use the point of the weapon, the arm should be extended; think of the blade as an extension of your forearm, a sort of long forefinger. Follow up the extension with the lunge. Make the point attack to the centre of the body, not too high or low. (see Figs. 12 and 13, pp. 75 and 77).

A variation of the lunge is the *Pass*, where the attacker steps forward with his rear foot, left foot passing right. The *Balestra* attack can also be used, where the attacker makes a little jump forward, recovers his balance and then makes his lunge. The *Fleche*, on the other hand, is not under sufficient control for stage fighting. *Ducking*, under the cut to right or left shoulder, also makes for variety; and here the attacker should make his cut high above the head of his opponent. If the duck is properly timed this safety precaution will pass unnoticed. Jumping over a low cut is also a good move and here again the cut can be made a little short of the jumping legs. Side-stepping an attack by carrying back the left foot, and ducking down touching the ground with the fingers of the left hand in the *Three Feet* are also methods of adding variety to the fight.

Sword and Buckler or Sword and Shield

Here attacks to the head and the left flank may be parried by the shield or buckler. The flat of the attacking weapon should be used and the shield angled to catch the blow squarely. It is obvious that the material should be strong enough to stand up to the impact, and make the right sort of noise (see Fig. 9, pp. 64–65).

Rapier and Dagger

Here the parrying should be done with the dagger and the attack made with the sword. The dagger may be used point up or down and a Main-gauche type of dagger gives better protection for the hand. A safe type of parry with sword and dagger is to cross the two blades near the hilts and catch cuts at the head or shoulders in the cross. The arms should be straight and pushed away from the body, the crossed weapons making as wide an angle as possible to catch the attacking weapon. Thrusts at the body can also be pushed aside to right or left using the crossed weapons (see Figs, 11, 12 and 13, pp. 71–73, 75–7).

Sabre Triangles

Thinking in terms of cutting weapons—sequences using the direct attacks and defensive box in sabre can be very useful in arranging stage fights. The attacks are made at the flank, the right cheek, the head, the left cheek, the chest, and the sword arm. The first defensive triangle is Prime (first), covering the inside flank to the left, Quinte (fifth), defending the head, and Seconde (second), defending the outside flank, right. The second triangle covers Tierce (third), covering right flank and cheek, Quarte (fourth), covering left cheek and flank, and again Quinte (fifth), to cover head attacks.

Modern sabre is a very mobile and athletic game, and cuts are made lightly by extending the sword arm and using the fingers to flick on the blade. In stage fencing the process must be much slower, and the weapons must look dangerous; the cadence too must be varied to build up excitement for the climax. Bearing these points in mind, the use of the triangles with prop swords will help the actors to build sequences that will be acceptable to an audience.

Balestra attacks (a small jump and a lunge) and spring-
ing backward give variety to the movement; and provided
that the weapons are fairly light, obsolete moves like the
Molinello can be introduced to give a period flavour.
Molinello may be horizontal, diagonal, or vertical and
may be performed from immobility, or combined with a
lunge. It is really a circular cut, and blade, forearm and
point describe a circle or part of a circle.

CHAPTER III

QUARTER STAFF

Attack

BEND the knees slightly, advance the right foot. Hold the staff hands well apart, left hand over right hand under the staff, roll the wrists, the elbows and the shoulders. Slide the pole through the hands to right or left and swing towards your opponent. Then pushing with the right arm and pulling with the left arm, swing the pole over towards your opponent's head. Then swing over to head—swing left to left flank then right to right flank. Head 1, left flank 2, right flank 3.

Now swing to head, allowing the pole to slip through the hands—recover and swing the pole to the outside of your opponent's right leg, allowing the pole to slip through the hands—now take a semi-circular swing towards the inside of your opponent's leg. Head 1, outside leg 2, inside leg 3.

Now practise Triangle 1, head, left flank, right flank; Triangle 2, head, outside leg, inside leg. Speed up with practice and then vary the sequences. Finally act the aggression but taking care to control the final stroke so that you can stop it before the strike reaches your opponent.

Defence

Bend the knees, advance the right or left foot. Hold the pole with the left hand over and the right hand under the pole—to defend the head lift the pole with both arms well above the head and slip under the pole. This is the invitation to a head swing from your opponent. Then

[continued on p. 29

Fig. 5a

Fig. 5b

Fig. 5. Quarter Staff.
(a) Hold the staff lightly, right hand under, left hand over. Roll from the shoulders.
(b) White steps forward and, letting the staff slip through his hands, attacks Black. Black covers his head by lifting his staff and stepping underneath.

Fig. 5c

Fig. 5d

(c) Black attacks White's left flank with a step forward. White parries by bringing his right hand up and carrying the staff across his body.
(d) Black swings his staff round and attacks White's right flank. White carries his staff from left to right, and parries.

Fig. 5e

Fig. 5f

(e) Black swings his staff again to right flank, and attacks with a lunge. White again carries his staff from right to left, and parries left flank.
(f) White steps forward and makes an attack on Black's left leg. Black stabs his staff into the ground and parries.

Fig. 5g

(g) White lets his staff slip through his hands from inside flank to attack outside flank—Black's right. Black lifts his staff over from left to right to parry the attack.

Remember—that by the *Invitation* method, the defender places his weapon in position before the attack is delivered. With practice the process is speeded up so that the audience is unaware that the vital place is covered, before the attack is launched.

bring the left hand down and extend both arms sideways to the right which invites a swing at the outside flank. Carry both extended arms over to defend the left flank. Then invite Triangle—head, right flank and left flank. Now defend head again; then loosen the left hand and stab the end of the pole into the ground to defend the outside right leg. Lift the end of the pole over and stab into the ground on the inside to defend the inside right leg. Then parry Triangle 2—Head; outside leg; lift over and defend inside leg. Recover the pole with the left hand over again ready for attack or defence. Vary the sequences of invitation and time the strokes for variation. Act the ferocity of the attack.

Robin Hood Plays and Pageants

From the experience of a wide variety of pageants, the usual order of things is that they turn into a dress parade without very much action. The most successful event in my experience was a historical pageant with a large number of mounted participants and the final scene consisted of all the mounted actors, some two hundred of them, forming up and trotting, then galloping, then easing to a trot before leaving the ring. This was a wild and exciting event and was certainly spectacular, probably reminiscent of the type of pageant mounted by the aristocracy in the time of Charles I and II. The other memorable incident was a confrontation between a Roman Army and Britain where the space allowed the Romans to form up shield to shield and advance rather like a modern tank attack, and they were harried by screaming Ancient Britons led by Queen Boadicea in her war chariot.

School plays are usually concerned with historical scenes in and around the area of the school. A very popular and successful scene can be mounted with Robin Hood and his outlaws of Sherwood in which wrestling matches and quarterstaff fights or even sword and buckler can be introduced with a fairground population as a background. A Horsefair is also a useful part of such an event. Gypsies make a colourful group and fit into most periods and knife fights between two King gypsies egged on by their followers can be exciting. Coming on to the Tudor period where rich and poor farmers can attend an annual fair with items such as dancing bears, the introduction of a fight, either as a trial by combat or two opposing family groups, can build up the scene. Georgian scenes can be made exciting by highwaymen either accosting travellers or in one instance, a captured highwayman was being driven to the gallows in the death cart, complete with coffin and soldiers marching on each side, when a rescue was contrived by three other highwaymen—one stopping the cart, the other diverting the soldiers and the third helping the captured highwayman to escape. Swords and pistols are used in this incident and the clashes and bangs and speed of the encounter can be made very exciting. Seventeenth- and eighteenth-century incidents can also be improved by the introduction of "gladiators" on a rostrum challenging all comers to quarterstaff, sword and buckler, back sword and small sword fights.

There is no question that pageants are made interesting and exciting by scenes with activity; and the introduction of a fight, using various weapons to fit in with the particular period, makes the whole thing more spectacular.

CHAPTER IV

TWO-HANDED SWORD

Mummer Play of St. George and the Dragon

This particular play involves a variety of stage fights. St. George is usually portrayed as a medieval knight and his opponents are the Giant Slasher Knight, the Turkish Knight; and there is a comedy sequence involving a Country Clown. The Master of Ceremonies, who is sometimes a jester and sometimes Father Christmas, calls in the characters who arrive and strike an attitude. The first character to be called in is Slasher Knight, who should be tall, is usually encased in some form of armour and uses a two-handed sword. He makes his boastful challenge flourishing the weapon. St. George is then called forth and on this occasion he too is armed with a two-handed sword and speaks his defiance of the challenge. The actual fight begins with St. George inviting the Slasher Knight to strike at his head by crouching and holding the sword upward and outward, and Slasher Knight steps forward and strikes his sword. Great care should be taken not to pull the attack and the practice of stopping the weapon should have been carried out. The actual blow is a light one, just enough to cause the necessary metal ring. St. George then takes up the attack and is invited to strike at both shoulders, right and left, outside and inside, and Slasher Knight holds his sword upright and to the right, upright and to the left. Slasher then takes up the attack and swings his sword down towards the right flank and is invited to do so by St. George, holding his sword point downwards, over to the right and then over to the left, catching the swing of Slasher's attack in both directions.

St. George then reverses his sword and with the pommel, holding the upper part of the blade and the cross-bar, strikes the Slasher Knight's helmet and he falls to the ground. Obviously the fight should be made as fierce as possible by growls and grunts on the attack and by a considerable amount of jockeying for position, rather like two boxers.

The next to be called forth is the fight between St. George and the Turkish Knight. The Turkish Knight is dressed in a turban, has curled pointed shoes and looks as eastern as possible, holding a curved scimitar and a round shield. St. George on this occasion also steps forward with a pointed shield and a shorter single-handed, cross-hilted sword. Once again the challenges are made and the battle commences with the Turkish Knight making a screaming attack aimed at the head, the right side of the neck and the left side of the neck. This is invited by St. George placing his weapon up and across and to the right and to the left (head, outside neck and inside neck). St. George follows this with an attack to the head and outside and inside leg which is invited by the Turkish Knight. St. George then lunges forward with the weapon pointed at the Turkish Knight's chest who runs his weapon along the blade into the two cross-bars making a corps-a-corps and they both wrestle. They break with a searing of the sword blade and St. George then makes a second thrust. The method is to place the blade along the Turkish Knight's right side, the Turkish Knight raising his weapon to enable this to happen, and apparently running through. The Turkish Knight sits down, overcome. When he is revived by the Doctor, the Turkish Knight should rise, kneeling; and, with his left hand holding the shield down and reversing the blade so that it makes a crucifix, he is raised up by St. George.

The Master of Ceremonies now calls forward the

[continued on p. 37

Fig. 6a

Fig. 6b

Fig. 6. Two-Handed Sword
(a) The grip, with the index finger round the crossbar. The blade is manipulated by the push and pull of the hands.
(b) All the energy and weight goes into the back swing, and the forward movement is under control and can be stopped if necessary.

Fig. 6c

Fig. 6d

(c) White, a step forward, swing and cut at head, parried by Black.
(d) Black parries to the right, White steps forward and swings an attack to right outside.

Fig 6e

Fig. 6f

(e) Black parries to the left inside, and meets the attack from White, swinging in from the right.

(f) A low attack at the inside leg by Black, parried by White who swings his defending blade from high to low line.

Fig. 6g

(g) Black reverses his hands and swings his two-edged blade over to attack outside the leg. This is parried by White.

Dragon but instead the Country Clown appears mouthing and tumbling and proceeds to bait and challenge St. George with a small poniard. St. George shows his contempt by turning his back and is stabbed by the Clown in the buttocks. St. George becomes very angry, flourishes his sword and chases the Country Clown who proceeds to run on the spot: this is done by advancing the right foot twelve inches, raising the left heel and drawing back the right foot parallel with the left foot. The left foot is then advanced, the right heel raised and the left foot drawn back parallel with the right foot and so on.

St. George slaps the Country Clown with the flat of his sword and on each slap he proceeds forward in a circle. In the end he falls down and tucks his head and arms in and receives a final slap on the buttocks and stretches out ready to be revived in a comic fashion by the Doctor.

D

Final Confrontation between St. George and the Dragon

The Dragon appears, roars loudly and rushes at St. George, who springs lightly aside. The Dragon then turns and rushes at him again with claws upraised and again St. George evades. Finally, the Dragon rushes straight forward on to St. George who places his sword on the side, as stated, and runs him through. On this occasion when the Dragon appeals for his life, after being revived, he is finally despatched by St. George.

At the conclusion of the play and just before the mock collection:—

Johnny Jack and Bellsie Bob, the black devil, have a light-hearted quarterstaff fight. Johnny Jack invites a blow to the head by lifting the quarterstaff high and keeping his hands well separated and Bellsie Bob bounces the staff by sliding it forward. Johnny Jack invites a blow to the shoulder by holding his staff to the right and then to the left and Bellsie Bob swings his staff left and right. Bellsie Bob then invites a head blow by lifting his staff and two cuts at the right leg by his opponent by dropping the end of the staff on to the ground to the right and then to the left. Finally, they press the centre of the staves together and push and wrestle and separate laughing. Johnny Jack, Bellsie Bob and Jerry Doubt then put collecting tins on the end of their staves and proceed to make a collection right and left with Johnny Jack in the centre.

ST. GEORGE AND THE DRAGON

CHARACTERS

JESTER
LITTLE JERRY DOUBT
SLASHER
ST. GEORGE
DOCTOR
TURKISH KNIGHT
CLOWN
DRAGON
BELLSIE BOB
JOHNNY JACK
THREE PRINCESSES (non-speaking)
SINGERS

[*Parade of fighters and clowns to suitable music.*]
[*Action line-up and* JESTER *steps forward.*]

JESTER *and*
   SINGERS:
(*Spoken and
   Sung*)

You gentle lords and ladies,
   of high and low, I say,
We all desire your favour
   To see our pleasant play.

Our play it is the best, sirs,
   That you would like to know;
And we will do our best, sirs,
   And think it well bestowed.

Though some of us be little
   And some a middle sort,
We all desire your favour
   To see our pleasant sport.

> You must not view our actions
> > Our wits are all to seek,
> So pray take no exceptions
> > At what we are going to speak.

JESTER (*waving the* SINGERS *away to the back of the stage*):

> Room, room, brave gallants all there,
> Pray give us room to rhyme;
> We've come to show a pageant
> This merry Summer-time.

LITTLE JERRY DOUBT (*running round after the* JESTER *and sweeping the stage*):

> Room, room,
> For me and my broom!

JESTER: Room, gentlemen, room, I pray,
> And we'll quickly have the fighting men
> > this way.
> (*He goes to the door to call in the fighting men.*)

SCENE I

JESTER: Step in, Bold Slasher.

Fanfare (2) [*Enter the* SLASHER KNIGHT, *in armour, carrying a huge sword.*]

SLASHER (*boastfully*):

> Here come I, Bold Slasher.
> I am a giant knight.
> I come to challenge bold St. George,
> To see if he will fight;
> He fights for old England,
> I'll soon knock him down;
> I'll break his head and tear his limbs
> And carry off his crown

JESTER (*at the door*):

> Step in, St. George.

Fanfare (3)   [*Enter* St. George, *carrying a two-handed sword. He has a breastplate, perhaps, but otherwise is not in armour.*]

St. George: Here come I, St. George, a worthy knight.

I'll spend my blood for England's right.
England's right I will maintain,
I'll fight for Old England once again.
Show me the man that bids me stand,
I'll cut him down with my courageous hand.

[*The two* Knights *confront each other defiantly.*]

Slasher: My head is made of iron,
My body is made of steel
My arms and legs of beaten brass;
No man can make me feel.

St. George: Stand off, stand off, Bold Slasher,
And let no more be said;
For if I draw my sword
I'm sure to break thy head.

Thou speakest very bold,
To such a man as I;
I'll cut thee into eyelet holes,
And make thy buttons fly!

So draw thy sword and fight,
Or draw thy purse and pay:
For satisfaction I must have
Before I go away.

Slasher: No satisfaction thou shalt have,
But I will bring thee to thy grave.

St. George: Battle to battle with thee I call,
To see who on this ground shall fall.

Slasher: Battle to battle with thee I pray
To see who on this ground shall lay.

ST. GEORGE: Then guard thy body and mind thy head,
                Or else my sword shall strike thee dead.

SLASHER: One shall die and the other shall live;
                This is the challenge that I do give.

(*Cymbal roll*)   [*They fight*, SLASHER *falls*.]

JESTER (*coming forward and addressing the audience*):
(*Doctor's   Is there a doctor to be found,
  tune*)   Or any near at hand,
                To heal this deep and deadly wound,
                And make the Slasher stand?

                [*Enter the* DOCTOR—*in black gown and three-cornered hat, carrying a bottle and bag.*]

DOCTOR: Yes, here's a doctor to be found,
                All ready near at hand,
                To heal this deep and deadly wound,
                And make the Slasher stand.

JESTER (*inquiring into his credentials*):
                Where hast thou been and where hast come from?

DOCTOR: Italy, Sicily, Germany, France and Spain:
                Three times round the world and back again.

JESTER: What canst thou do and what canst cure?

DOCTOR: All sorts of ills and sicknesses
                Just what my physic please;
                The itch, stitch, palsy and the gout,
                Pains in and pains without.

JESTER: What is thy fee, doctor?

DOCTOR: Now fifteen pounds, it is my fee,
                The money to lay down.
                But as 'tis such a rogue as he,
                I'll cure him for ten pounds.

JESTER: Try thy skill, doctor.

DOCTOR (*kneeling down by the* SLASHER):

> I have a bottle by my side;
> The fame spreads far and wide.
> A drop on head, a drop on heart—
> [*He rises to his feet.*]
> Rise up, and take thy part.
> [*He goes out.* SLASHER *rises.*]

SLASHER (*kneeling, as* ST. GEORGE *advances threateningly.*)

> O pardon, pardon, St. George!
> One thing of thee I crave;
> Spare me my life, and I
> Will be thy constant slave.

ST. GEORGE: Yes, proud Slasher, but arise,
>   And go and tell thy land
>   What a bold champion now
>   In England there doth stand.

> [SLASHER *goes out—or joins the* SINGERS *at the
> back of the stage.*]

LITTLE
JERRY DOUBT (*running round with his broom and sweeping up
    after the fight*):

> Room, room,
> For me and my broom.

ST. GEORGE: Here stand I, St. George,
>   A champion am I.
>   I'll fight with any heathen knight
>   And his cold courage try.
>   I'll give my life for England's right,
>   A challenge now I cry.

> [*Step in the* TURKISH KNIGHT (*curved sword
> and round shield*) *with* THREE PRINCESSES.]

| TURKISH KNIGHT: | Here come I the heathen knight
Come from foreign lands to fight,
I come to fight St. George
The man of courage bold,
And if his blood be hot,
I soon will make it cold. |

| ST. GEORGE: | I'll fight with thee
Thou heathen knight.
So gird thyself
And boldly fight. |

[*They fight.* TURKISH KNIGHT *falls.*]

JESTER (*coming forward and addressing the audience*):

| (*Doctor's tune*) | Is there a doctor to be found,
Or any near at hand,
To heal this deep and deadly wound,
And make the Turkish Knight stand? |

[*Enter the* DOCTOR—*in black gown and three-cornered hat, carring a bag and bottle.*]

| DOCTOR: | Yes, here's a doctor to be found
All ready near at hand,
To heal this deep and deadly wound,
And make the Turkish Knight stand. |

DOCTOR (*kneeling down by the* TURKISH KNIGHT):

I have a bottle by my side;
The fame spreads far and wide.
A drop on head, a drop on heart—

[*He rises to his feet.*]

Rise up, and take thy part.

[*He goes out.* TURKISH KNIGHT *rises.*]

| TURKISH KNIGHT: | O! pardon, pardon, St. George,
One thing of thee I pray.
Spare me my life
And I will give thee
All my slaves. |

St. George: Arise O Gallant Turkish Knight
And go and tell thy land
Christian St. George has won the day
Against him none can stand.
Let your slaves go free for me
And dance to make us gay.
[Princesses *dance*.]

[Turkish Knight *kneels, holds up his sword
by the blade to make a cross, rises and exits with
the* Princesses.]

Scene ii

Jester (*coming forward*):

Proceed, St. George.

St. George: Here stand I, St. George; from Britain did I
spring,
Now I'll fight the Dragon bold, my wonders
to begin
I'll clip his wings, he shall not fly;
I'll cut him down, or else I die.

Jester (*at the door*):

Step in, bold Dragon.

[*To the evident astonishment of the* Jester *and*
St. George. *and the amusement of the* Singers,
there enters, not the Dragon but the Clown.
*He wears his wooden dagger and carries a pipe,
whistle, or mouth-organ.*]

Clown (*as he bounds in*):

Here comes I, as ain't been yet,
With my big head and little wit,
My head so big, my wit so small,
I will dance a jig to please you all.

[*He dances; perhaps sings too. Then, seeing* ST.
GEORGE *advancing wrathfully, he draws his
dagger and confronts the knight.*]

I am a valiant hero, lately come from sea,
You never saw me before, now did you?
I slew ten men with a seed of mustard,
Ten thousand with an old crushed toad.
What do you think of that, Sir Saint?
If you don't be off I'll serve you the same.

ST. GEORGE: I'll hash you, and smash you, as small as
      flies,
     And send you to Jamaica to make mince-
      pies.

CLOWN: You'll hash me, and smash me, as small as
      flies,
     And send me to Jamaica to make mince-
      pies.

     [*They fight. The* CLOWN *falls.*]

JESTER (*coming forward*):
     Is there a doctor to be found,
     Or any near at hand,
     To heal this deep and deadly wound,
     And make this fellow stand?
     [*Enter the* DOCTOR, *as before.*]

DOCTOR: Yes, here's a doctor to be found,
     All ready near at hand,
     To heal this deep and deadly wound,
     And make this fellow stand.

JESTER: Where hast thou been and where hast thou
     come from?

DOCTOR: I have travelled from my old grandmother's
fireside to her bread-and-cheese cupboard,
and there had many a rare piece of bread and
cheese.

JESTER: What canst thou do and what canst cure?

DOCTOR: All sorts of ills and sicknesses.
            Just what my physic please;
            The itch, stitch, palsy and the gout;
            A devil I'll get out.

JESTER: What is thy fee, doctor?

DOCTOR: Now fifteen pounds, it is my fee,
            The money to lay down.
            But as 'tis such a fool as he,
            I'll cure for half-a-crown.

JESTER: Try thy skill, doctor.

DOCTOR (*kneeling down by the* CLOWN):

            I will feel this man's pulse (*pulse noise*);
            [*He feels for the pulse in the elbow or ankle.*]
            Very bad, very bad indeed!
            Take a little of this medicine.
            This man is not dead but in a trance.
            Arise, my lad, and take a dance.

(*Clown's dance*)

            [*He goes out. The* CLOWN *rises and dances again
            and then goes out, or joins the* SINGERS *at the
            back of the stage.*]

LITTLE JERRY DOUBT (*running round again and sweeping up
the stage after the fight*):

            Room, room,
            For me and my broom!

                        SCENE 3

JESTER (*coming forward*):

            Proceed, St. George.

ST. GEORGE (*making a fresh start after the* CLOWN'S *interruption*):   Here stand I, St. George; from Britain did I spring.

I'll fight the Dragon, now, my wonders to begin.

I'll clip his wings, he shall not fly;

I'll cut him down, or else I die!

JESTER (*hopefully*):

Step in, bold Dragon.

(*Drum roll*)   [*Enter the* DRAGON, *roaring fiercely.*]

DRAGON: Who's he that seeks the Dragon's blood,

And calls so angry and so loud?

That English dog, will he before me stand?

I'll cut him down with my courageous hand.

With my long teeth and scurvy jaw.

Of such I'd break up half a score.

And stay my stomach, till I'd more.

[ST. GEORGE *confronts the* DRAGON *boldly.*]

ST. GEORGE: Battle to battle with thee I call,

To see who on this ground shall fall.

DRAGON: Battle to battle with thee I pray,

To see who on this ground shall lay.

ST. GEORGE: Then guard thy body and mind thy head,

Or else my sword shall strike thee dead.

DRAGON: One shall die and the other shall live;

This is the challenge that I do give.

[*They fight, and the* DRAGON *falls.*]

JESTER (*coming forward and addressing the audience*):

Is there a doctor to be found,

Or any near at hand,

To heal this deep and deadly wound,

And make the Dragon stand?

[*Enter the* DOCTOR, *as before.*]

DOCTOR: Yes, here's a doctor to be found
All ready near at hand,
To heal this deep and deadly wound,
And make the Dragon stand.

JESTER: Where hast thou been and where hast thou
come from?

DOCTOR: Italy, Sicily, Germany, France and Spain;
Three times round the world and back
again.

JESTER: What canst thou do and what canst cure?

DOCTOR: All sorts of ills and sicknesses
Just what my physic please;
The itch, stitch, palsy and the gout,
Pains in and pains without.

JESTER: What is thy fee, doctor?

DOCTOR: Now fifteen pounds, it is my fee,
The money to lay down.
But as 'tis such a rogue as he,
I'll cure him for ten pounds.

JESTER: Try thy skill, doctor.

DOCTOR (*kneeling beside the* DRAGON):

I have a bottle by my side;
The fame spreads far and wide.
A drop on head, a drop on heart—
[*He stands up.*]
Rise up, and take thy part.
[*He goes out.*]

DRAGON (*raising his head as* ST. GEORGE *advances*):

O pardon, pardon, St. George;
One thing of thee I crave;
Spare me my life, and I
Will be thy constant slave.

ST. GEORGE: No, no, that may not be;
             For thus is the story told,
             That now the brave St. George
             Did slay the Dragon bold.

                         [*He kills the* DRAGON. ST. GEORGE *and the*
(*cheer*)   JESTER *remove the* DRAGON *to the side of the*
                         stage.]

LITTLE JERRY DOUBT (*running round and sweeping up after the*
   fight):   Room room,
                         For me and my broom!

JESTER (*coming forward and addressing the audience*):
                         Ladies and gentlemen, our sport is done,
                         We can no longer stay,
                         Remember, now, that ever more
(*cheer*)   St. George will hold the sway.

                         Ladies and gentlemen, we dare to hope,
                         If you've enjoyed our play,
                         That you will now give to our cause
                         As freely as you may.

                         [*He turns to call the collectors*—BELLSIE BOB,
                         JOHNNY JACK *and* LITTLE JERRY DOUBT.]
                         Step forward, my merry men.

                         [*The three collectors come forward in turn with
                         their bags.*]

BELLSIE BOB (*his club over his shoulder, his can in his hand*):
                         Here come I, old Bellsie Bob.
                         On my shoulder I carry a club.
                         In my hand an empty can—
                         Don't you think I'm a jolly old man?

JOHNNY JACK (*with his family of rag dolls on his back*):
                         Here come I, Johnny Jack,
                         With all my family at my back!

My family's large and I am small;

(*Wassail*   A little, if you please, will help us all.
  during   [BELLSIE BOB *and* JOHNNY JACK *fight quarter-*
  collection)   *staff to a laughing and panting conclusion.*]

LITTLE JERRY DOUBT (*with his broom and bag*):

Here come I, little Jerry Doubt.

If you don't give me money I'll sweep you
out.

Money I want and money I pray;

If you don't give me money I'll sweep you
away!

[*Parade off.*]

PRINCESS IDA

A version of a fight to music, between the three Princes
and the three Knights (see score, Fig. 7, pp. 54–8).

CHARACTERS

PRINCE HILARION (son of KING HILDEBRAND)
PRINCE CYRIL
PRINCE FLORIAN
KING GAMA
THREE KNIGHTS (sons of King Gama):
    ARAC, GURON and SCYNTHIUS
PRINCESS IDA (daughter of KING GAMA)
THREE LADIES: BLANCHE, PSYCHE and
    MELISSA
SOLDIERS

GAMA: If I were not the Princess Ida's father,
And so had not her brothers for my sons,
No doubt you'd wring my neck—in safety too!
Come, come, Hilarion, begin, begin![1]

[1] Supers take away sticks from their arms. The three undo their robes
and step out of them. Supers take robes and sticks off L. Swords are handed
to the three Princes by the soldiers nearest.

Give them no quarter—they will give you none.
You've this advantage over warriors
Who kill their country's enemies for pay—
You know what you are fighting for—look there!
(*Pointing to Ladies on the battlements.*)[1]
(*Desperate fight between the three* PRINCES *and the three* KNIGHTS, *during which the ladies on the battlements and the* SOLDIERS *on the stage sing the following chorus*):

This is our duty plain towards
    Our Princess all immaculate
We ought to bless her brothers' swords,
    And piously ejaculate:
      Oh, Hungary!
      Oh, Hungary!
    Oh, doughty sons of Hungary!
      May all success
      Attend and bless
    Your warlike ironmongery!
    Hilarion! Hilarion! Hilarion!

(*By this time* ARAC, GURON *and* SCYNTHIUS *are on the ground, wounded*—HILARION, CYRIL *and* FLORIAN *stand over them.*)

PRINCESS (*entering through gate and followed by Ladies and* HILDEBRAND):[2] Hold! Stay your hands!—We yield ourselves to you![3]

    Ladies, my brothers all lie bleeding there![4]
    Bind up their wounds—but look the other way

END OF FIGHT

[1] GAMA up centre.

[2] IDA enters Centre, followed by BLANCHE, PSYCHE and MELISSA, HILDEBRAND enters Centre, GAMA is on and disappointed at the result. PSYCHE goes down to CYRIL Left, MELISSA to FLORIAN Right.

[3] Ladies come down from rostrum, soldiers off Centre and on rostrum from back. All changes must be done very quietly.

[4] IDA goes to GURON Left.

The fight is essentially a musical piece and the movement and clashing of the weapons must be timed so that they fit into the musical sequence.

The contestants are the three Princes against the three Knights and each one is armed with a two-handed sword. Before the fight they throw off their heavy armour to enable them to move effectively.

Positions for start of Mock Heroic Fight

Arac : Cyril   Scynthius : Florian
Guron : Hilarion

The same sequence is carried out by each couple, and in time to the music. All the power goes into the back swing and forward cuts must be controlled and stopped if necessary. Cuts should be made at right and left shoulders and right and left thighs.

Bars 1–4   Limbering up and salute, lift swords. Both hands to chin and lower first to ladies and then to opponents.
Bars 5–8   Princes attack right and left shoulders of Knights. Knights parry.
Bars 9–12   Knights attack right and left thighs of Princes. Princes parry.
Bars 13–16 Princes attack right shoulders and right thighs of Knights and Knights parry.
Bars 17–20 Knights attack left shoulders and right shoulders of Princes.
Bars 21–24 Princes and Knights run sword hilts together in a corps-a-corps and wrestle and break with a clashing of weapons. Change opponents.
Bars 25–28 Arac to Florian.
            Guron to Cyril.
            Arac to Hilarion.
Bars 29–32 Princes attack right and left thighs of Knights. Knights parry.

E

Bars 33–36 Princes attack right shoulders and right thighs of Knights. Knights parry.

Bars 37–40 Knights attack right and left shoulders of Princes. Princes parry.

Bars 41–43 Princes swing swords round at Knights' heads —Knights duck.

Bars 44–46 Knights swing swords round low at Princes' feet—Princes jump over blades.

Bars 46–55 Knights hold swords over heads and Princes
to end of   hammer opponents' guards down. Knights
music   subside to kneeling position and finally fall.
       Princes place one foot each on opponents and
       lift swords in triumph.

PRINCESS IDA *enters centre*

CHORUS DURING THE FIGHT

Cue: (Gama): "You know what you are fighting for – look there!"

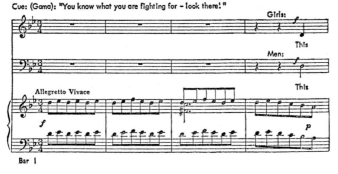

Fig. 7. Princess Ida (fight score)

208

209

sons   of   Hun — ga — ry!

sons   of   Hun — ga — ry!

Bar 30

May   all   suc — cess   At — tend   and

May   all   suc — cess   At — tend   and

Bar 34

bless   Your   war — like   i   —   ron — mon — ge

bless   Your   war — like   i , —   ron — mon — ge

Bar 38

(17181)

CHAPTER V

ROMAN FIGHTS AND BATTLE SCENES

VEGETIUS the Roman military historian, commenting on methods of attack, says "A slash-cut rarely kills, however powerfully delivered, because the vitals are protected by the enemy's weapons and also by his bones. A thrust, going in two inches, however, can be fatal; and you must penetrate the vitals to kill a man. Moreover, when a man is slashing, the right side and arm are left bare. When thrusting, however, the body is covered (by the Roman shield) and the enemy is wounded before he knows what has happened."

This gives some idea of the Roman approach to wars: no individual combat, no shouting berserk; just sheer dogged tank-like battle and advance. And although the officers dressed in plumed helmets, and moulded and chiselled breastplates, and had gold and silver inlay on their weapons, the legionary with his round helmet and cheek-guards, marching sandals, stout shirt and sweat-cloth round his neck, kilt and woollen breeches, is hardly a romantic figure; his shoulders and chest guarded by strip armour, and the large rectangular shield made of wood and covered with leather, protect him, and his weapons are a seven-foot throwing spear (the *pilum*) and a short-pointed two-edged sword (the *gladius*). Keeping behind the shield the legionary would bring up the point of his weapon smartly towards his opponent's face.

From the stage point of view it is necessary to consider the acting space as a small part of the field, where incidents will take place: at times it will be filled with a moving mass; sometimes empty, as the battle is carried to another part of the field; again small fighting groups will be in-

Fig. 8. Moulton County Primary School historical pageant.

volved. If spectators are involved as in *Romeo and Juliet*, the scene must be kept moving and interest directed from one fighting group to another. The atmosphere of battle can be created by the waving of banners, smoke, and cries and clashes off-stage, and in a Roman play like *Julius Caesar* full use should be made of the confrontations between the opposing armies, where the soldiers of both sides file in and make way for their leaders, who meet to exchange parley or abuse, before leaving for the battle. The stage picture can be greatly improved by the use of levels, and movable rostra; ramps and steps can also make the actual fights more dramatic.

Suicide, rather than suffer dishonourable submission, and the denigration of public exhibition, is a feature of some Roman plays. The last scene in *Julius Caesar* is concerned with the self-inflicted death of the noble Brutus—

BRUTUS: I pr'ythee, Strato, stay thou by thy lord;
Thou art a fellow of a good respect;
Thy life hath had some smatch of honour in it:
Hold, then, my sword, and turn away thy face,
While I do run upon it. Wilt thou, Strato?

STRATO: Give me thy hand first: fare thee well, my good
lord.

BRUTUS: Farewell, good Strato.
Caesar, now be still:
I killed not thee with half so good a will.

Here Brutus must offer his drawn sword, hilt first to his
slave Strato, who receives it, passes it from right hand to
left for the Roman handshake. He then takes the sword
firmly in his right hand, and places the point against
Brutus' side, away from the audience. Bring the blade in
flat against the side to ensure that it does not catch in the
clothes of the opponent. Brutus then places both hands
on the shoulders of Strato, and as he drives the blade forward, seemingly into the body, he must react and retract
as if he was receiving the point in his vitals. The expres-
sion on his face, too, is important, and a blood capsule,
as supplied by Leichner, may be bitten to produce a blood
issue from the mouth, to add realism to the action. Finally
Strato must withdraw the sword, with a definite effort—
it is easier to stab in the weapon than to get it out; and as
he does so, Brutus falls forward on to his face.

CHAPTER VI

SWORD AND BUCKLER

IN all cases a right-handed swordsman is envisaged, and with this particular period in mind, the sword should be worn on the left side, and should hang vertically down. A "Frog" from the belt would be helpful, or the belt could hang obliquely from above the right hip. The buckler, which was gripped in the left hand and did not hang from the shoulder like a shield, varied in size from the circumference of a small plate, to that of a Highland targe. The rough idea was to hold it high when the sword was attacking low, and vice versa.

Fighting with the sword tended to be extremely rough and there was no system of attack as in modern sabre play. No defined guards existed, and the result depended upon physical agility. The fighters stayed out of distance, circling round each other rather like boxers until they saw an opening, then rushed in with a shout to put the opponent off guard. The edge of the blade was used with a chopping motion, and all defence was with the buckler, sword cuts being deflected. Side-stepping, wrestling, tripping, use of the sword hilt, and striking with the buckler were all acceptable.

Make the fight vocal, and fierce, and aim your blows at your opponent, not past him.

Use of the Rapier

In holding the weapon, grip the quillon or cross-bar with the index finger, rather like holding a pistol. If the dagger is used, attacks should be made with the sword and the dagger used mainly for deflecting the opponent's sword. The dagger should be gripped with the left hand and the point either upwards or downwards is acceptable. Attacks can be beaten off more easily with the point upwards. Crossing the sword and dagger, too, either above the head or to the flank, is a safe and easy way of catching a cut from the opponent's sword.

The rapier is predominantly a thrusting weapon, but earlier rapiers were also cutting weapons. There were recognised attacks and guards, but side-stepping and agility in general dictated the fight, and the opponents kept out of distance, lunging or running in as an opening appeared, parrying all counter-attacks with the dagger.

Two rapiers were sometimes used, or a cloak, wrapped twice round the forearm, leaving a hanging piece which was used to envelope the opponent's blade, could also take the place of the dagger for defence.

The sword was frequently carried attached to a decorative bandolier, and hung balanced out behind. As weapons were sometimes six feet long, this balance was very necessary.

The fighters should move round each other, looking for an opening, and the swords are never in contact or engaged, at the opening of the fight.

The Small Sword

This decorative little weapon was carried on a belt worn across the hips, or sometimes suspended from hooks at the back of the skirted coat. The position of On-guard was very wide, with the weight on the left leg. The sword arm was well extended with the elbow only slightly bent —an exaggeration of the present position in modern fencing. Lunges, too were very long, and the parries consisted of *Prime, Seconde, Quarte and Tierce*. Wide circular movements were popular, but the mode of fight was defined, if not always adhered to. The left hand was sometimes used to parry, and side-stepping and displacements

Fig. 9a

Fig. 9b

Fig. 9. Sword and Buckler

(a) White makes an attack with the flat of the sword and guards high with the buckler. Black makes a high parry with the buckler, and waits a chance to attack.

(b) Both Black and White foil flank attacks (made with the flat for sound and safety.)

Fig. 9c

Fig. 9d

(c) A crouching attack by Black, and a parry of a head cut from White.
(d) A full arm parry by Black; White attacking at left leg, with a down
swing.

of the body were also popular. The *Pass* was often used instead of lunging, and disarming was taught and practised. There is a close kinship in the use of this weapon and our modern ideas of fencing, and skill and finesse are necessary in a stage fight with the small sword (see Fig. 14, pp. 84–86).

Opening Scene, 'Romeo and Juliet'

The scene is an open square in Verona with a market group and passers-by conversing and moving in Elizabethan style with manipulation of swords and wide skirts.

The scene opens with the arrival of Sampson and Gregory, two of the Capulet clan, and there is immediate reaction of dislike and fear from the stallholders and passers-by. The two men approach in a swashbuckling manner and there is an altercation between Sampson and one of the stall women who slaps his face. This calls for raucous laughter from Gregory and the opening words of the play are spoken. The two men continue to exchange banter until the entry of Abraham and another, two of the Montagues. There follow the insults and the challenge, egged on by the arrival of Tybalt, and the four men, using sword and buckler, fight. Benvolio enters and endeavours to stop the fight by beating down the swords of two of the combatants, when Tybalt issues his challenge and all six proceed to fight—Tybalt and Benvolio with sword and dagger. The citizens enter with clubs and partisans and, egged on by the crowd, beat down the swords of Sampson, Gregory, Abraham and the other.

Old Capulet, dragged back by Lady Capulet, and old Montague, dragged by Lady Montague, enter from two sides and shout insults at each other; the noise of a drum is heard and Prince Escalus enters with his train and endeavours to quell the combatants, but he is not heard above the din until the shout of "Will you not hear". He then proceeds to lecture the warring families and threatens

Fig. 10. *Romeo and Juliet*. ROMEO (Patrick Marlow) beats down the swords of TYBALT (Rex Robinson) and MERCUTIO (Andrew Manley). Royal Theatre and Opera House, Northampton, October 1971. Director: Willard Stoker. Fight Director: Gilbert Gordon.

them with death, and all except Montague, Capulet and their ladies kneel and throw their distempered weapons to the ground on his command. He bids Capulet and Montague both meet him and bids all men to part on pain of death. He then exits centre, followed by his train; Capulet and his group depart left and Montague and his group depart to right to end the scene.

The sword fights are conducted on the basis of an invitation to attack. Under ordinary circumstances the defender has to anticipate where the attack will come. In a stage fight the procedure is for the defender to indicate the place of the attack. In the case of the serving men with the swords and bucklers, practice on the two sabre triangles should be carried out. Triangle 1 is the defence of the head and the right and left flank; Triangle 2 is the defence of the head and the right and left leg. These invitations may be given alternately and gradually and the practice speeded up. The actors must then time their strokes to get the necessary realism and excitement into the fight. A head cut and a duck can also be introduced and a cut at the leg which is jumped over.

With regard to the sword and dagger, Benvolio and Tybalt will be armed with cut and thrust rapiers and cuts should be parried by a crossing of the rapier and dagger. This cross invitation can again be to cover the head and the right and left flank. Attacks should be made with the sword and parries mainly with the dagger. Breathing space and pauses in the fight can be covered by a beat and counter-beat on the defender's extended blade. The culminating moment in the Benvolio and Tybalt fight should be a "corps à corps" when both blades are extended upwards, hilts are run together and the dagger hand brought over so that a wrestling match can take place.

CHAPTER VII

RAPIER AND DAGGER

The Fight Scene—'Hamlet'

THE fight scene in *Hamlet* is the exciting and physical ending to the play of words. It would have been acted by expert swordsmen in the presence of a company which understood fully what was being done. All the subtleties of the play would be fully appreciated by both the groundlings standing in the yard and the experts smoking their pipes on the stage.

Burbadge, of course, played Hamlet and Laertes was played by William Sly, who was the fiery young swordsman of the company and also played Hotspur and Tybalt. I think the best exposition on the fight is by Dover Wilson, and I would work largely to his explanation. The thing that has to be brought out is that Hamlet becomes aware of the plot against him when he is hit by the sharp used by Laertes, and decides to gain possession of it. I would say that at this moment he finally shakes off his irresolution and becomes the hero at bay.

The lead up to the fight scene is by young Osric who, in his flamboyant manner, brings the challenge. We have previously seen how the plot is laid between Laertes and the King, Claudius. The King tells Laertes that Hamlet is anxious to meet him in fence, having recently heard great things of his skill from a French visitor to the Danish Court. He proposes to bring them together for a wager, when "with ease, or with a little shuffling, you may choose a sword unbated, and in a pass of practice requite him for your father". Laertes, not to be outdone, suggests that he annoint the point of the weapon with a poison in his possession, so mortal "that if I gall him slightly it may be death". Claudius caps this with the project of the poisoned chalice, telling Laertes to attack furiously so that Hamlet, being thirsty between the bouts, will drink the poison in the chalice. Then to Hamlet comes young Osric saying, "The king, sir, hath laid, sir, that in a dozen passes between yourself and him [Laertes] he shall not exceed you three hits." (This means that Hamlet gets a start of three in the fight.) "He hath laid on twelve for nine." This means that Laertes, conscious of the heavy odds, has stipulated twelve bouts for the usual nine, which were customary in Shakespeare's time. Hamlet, having taken a rise out of Osric, accepts the conditions and is, quite evidently, by reason of his straightforward character, completely unaware that there is any dirty work afoot. He asks what is his weapon, that is, what sort of a fence does he propose, and Osric replies "rapier and dagger". It is interesting to note that when the first text of *Hamlet* was printed in 1623 no daggers are mentioned in the folio stage direction, the reason for this being presumably that sword and dagger had gone out of fashion and the long rapier, which was both a defensive and offensive weapon, had come in.

There is little doubt that a foile, which was nothing like our present Fleuret, was used. The foile in the play would be very similar to our épée, with a handguard and quillons, and the dagger would be a short weapon used for cutting and stabbing. A favourite piece of play in a duel was to cut the tendons of your opponent's leg with the dagger. When Hamlet was first staged, sword and buckler sword play was in vogue in England. This was a cutting and pointing weapon and the buckler could be anything from a very small hand buckler about the size of a plate, to the target used until 1745 by Highlanders in Scotland. The sword and cloak or long rapiers with the left hand covered

[continued on p. 74

Fig. 11a

Fig. 11b

Fig. 11. Rapier and Dagger (Cut and Thrust)
(a) A head cut by White parried with the dagger by Black, and a low thrust in Prime, parried with the dagger by White.
(b) An attempted sword and dagger thrust by Black, parried Prime and Seconde by White with sword and dagger.

Fig. 11c

Fig. 11d

(c) A parry of a head cut by Black and a Corps-a-Corps with both fighters holding and wrestling.
(d) A cut at head by White, parried by a cross guard of sword and dagger by Black.

Fig. 11e

Fig. 11f

(e) A cut at inside neck (Quarte side) by White, parried with the cross guard by Black.

(f) A cut at outside neck by Black (Sixte side) parried by the cross guard, sword and dagger, by White.

with a glove of mail were used to beat off the attack. Rapier play had recently been imported from abroad and the sword and buckler men were regarded as out of date, so that when Hotspur wants to be insulting about the Prince of Wales he calls him "that same sword and buckler Prince of Wales", indicating that he was a low fellow and out of date at that. Therefore the fight could be staged using sword and buckler, sword and cloak, rapier and dagger or just rapier, but it is ridiculous to use a modern small fencing foil and it is worth noting that this is usually done in stage productions. Modern methods of fence are a vast improvement on anything which was in vogue before the nineteenth century. The sword play of the time was largely a matter of strength and agility. It was quite in order to sieze your opponent and use wrestling tricks on him.

On the other hand, in staging the fight I think it is essential that the exchange of weapons should not develop into a vulgar scuffle. The usual procedure is to force a corps-a-corps and as a result the fencers drop their foils and when retrieving exchange weapons. This would indicate that Hamlet gets his revenge by pure accident, which I think was never intended by Shakespeare.

The progress of the fight is that foils are brought on by young Osric. Laertes is already prepared. As rapiers of that period could be used for cutting as well as pointing, even a bated buttoned weapon could give a nasty clout, and in all probability a small reinforced cap would be worn and possibly a shirt of mail. Hamlet can change for the fight in full view of the audience. Laertes, as I have said, is already changed. The business of choosing the unbated weapon is contrived by the King talking to Hamlet and while that happens Laertes says that he is dissatisfied with his weapon and goes over to choose another. I think it is fair to suggest that young Osric throughout is in the know or at any rate partially so, and is party to the unbated sword. After all, he is the man who was "put on" by the King to press the excellence of Laertes and lure Hamlet to the match. If Osric places the weapons on the side table after the first choice, it is then an easy matter for Laertes to indicate to the audience that he has chosen this special weapon and at the same time annoint it with the poison while Hamlet is kept in conversation with the King.

The match begins and Laertes takes the offensive, pressing Hamlet hard. Hamlet scores the first hit which is not acknowledged but is stated as a very palpable hit and Claudius appears to be pleased: kettle-drums beat, trumpets blow, and the canon is fired, indicating that the King's champion is successful. It is now that Claudius produces the cup of wine, holds up a magnificent pearl which he has given to Hamlet, and poisons the wine. However, when offered a drink Hamlet says, "I'll play this bout first". He also refuses the drink from the Queen. This is good sense

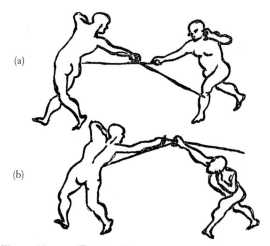

Fig. 12. Thrusts (*Fabris*) and Rapier and Dagger (*Capo Ferro*.)
(a) Thrust Seconde by a pass timed by disengage outside.
(b) Time thrust on feint of disengage.

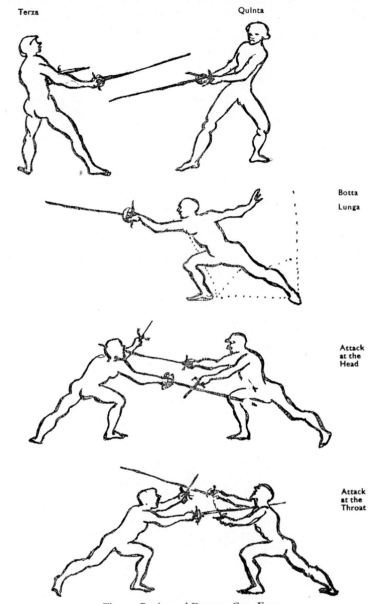

Fig. 12. Rapier and Dagger: *Capo Ferro*.

Secunda Guarda   Sesta Guarda

Fig. 13. Thrusts (*Fabris*) and Guards (*Capo Ferro*).
(a) Thrust in quarte counter parried with dagger.
(b) *Capo Ferro*. A—Quarta Guard; D—Prima Guard.
(c) *Capo Ferro*.

inasmuch as an athlete would know that drinking during a fight would cause him to sweat and slow him up. The second bout is engaged and Laertes redoubles his efforts, trying to wound Hamlet with the poisoned point or, alternatively, to keep him in vigorous motion so that he becomes "hot and dry". Hamlet scores again and the King realises that Laertes will be hard put to it to hit him. "Our son shall win" cries the King, pretending to be pleased. The Queen is, of course, delighted at the way her dear boy is holding his own: she goes to him during the interval and noticing that perspiration is trickling into his eyes—a bad thing for a fencer—she offers him her handkerchief and makes the remark about him being "fat and scant of breath". There is no shadow of doubt that this reference to perspiration is not a subtle barb from Shakespeare against the increasing fat of Dick Burbadge—no actor-manager would call attention to a defect in his leading actor. Once again Hamlet refuses the drink, saying in effect he will have it when he is certain of a victory, and then we have the business of the King, who is genuinely fond of Gertrude, watching her drink the poison. This, of course, is going to threaten the entire plot and to Laertes' "My lord, I'll hit him now" Claudius gives the gloomy reply, "I do not think't."

His doubts are justified by the third bout which ends in a draw and Hamlet, having taken Laertes' measure, rallies him on his vehement tactics—"You do but dally, I pray you pass with your best violence. I am afeared you make a wanton of me." Laertes attacks with more violence than ever, but unsuccessfully. The point of Laertes' weapon, as Hamlet wards off a particularly furious stroke, becomes jammed in the projecting hooks of the dagger, and judges intervene, part them with the announcement, "Nothing, neither way." Laertes is now desperate, the Queen is beginning to droop in her chair of state; Hamlet shows no sign of wishing to drink from the cup—three bouts have passed without his being even touched—so while Hamlet is off his guard Laertes suddenly lunges, shouting "Have at you now!" and wounds him in the arm. Hamlet must indicate that he has actually been hit by a sharp and I think that blood, visible to the audience, is a good idea. Determined to get possession of the sharp, Hamlet closes with Laertes and contrives the exchange. We will illustrate a number of methods of this exchange (see Figs. 19 and 20, pp. 94–99).

Hamlet now has the sharp, Claudius makes a last attempt to save his accomplice, shouting "Part them, they are incensed." Hamlet counters this, "Nay, come again", and before anyone can intervene he runs through Laertes. Laertes staggers back into Osric's arms dying, and the "brother's wager" is at an end.

CHAPTER VIII

POINT RAPIER

IN the heroic comedy by Edmond Rostand, *Cyrano de Bergerac*, there is an exciting duel scene where Cyrano, the great swordsman, who is sensitive about his very large nose, is insulted by a young nobleman, the Vicomte de Valvert. While fighting the duel Cyrano also composes a ballade—a poem of three verses of eight lines with an envoi of four lines.

Cyrano tosses aside his hat and cloak, and drawing his sword engages the Vicomte with a beat and counter-beat; in other words he taps the opposing blade sharply, and circles underneath to tap on the other side. Do this three or four times, moving forward and backward, keeping fencing distance. The Vicomte then launches an attack to the right flank, and this is parried by Cyrano, who disengages and puts him back on guard like a fencing master. The Vicomte beats and makes a pass attack high and low left; the move is countered by Cyrano's parry of quarte and septime. Cyrano steps back and makes his threat on the last line. Cyrano holds the Vicomte in play by beat, counter-beat and pressure as he opens his second verse, then makes a short lunge to the heart, eludes the parry and flicks the ribbons on the Vicomte's chest. He then beats and counter-beats and clashes the blades, and makes a one-two-three attack avoiding the parry each time. Once more he makes his threat by pointing the sword and stepping forward.

The Vicomte makes a rush forward which Cyrano avoids by stepping aside, then he turns and comes on guard facing the opposite way. He does a jump attack and drives the Vicomte back. The Vicomte lunges, steps up and makes a pass attack, Cyrano steps back and parries quarte, bears down on the blade, reaches out with his left hand and, turning the sword down and inwards with his right hand, catching the cup guard with his left, he snatches the weapon from the Vicomte's hand, reverses it, threatens and then tosses it back (see Figs. 19a, p. 94, and 20b, p. 99). The final verse threat is then made as usual. Cyrano now becomes very solemn, for the envoi.

The desperate Vicomte makes a final effort with a beat and attack right and left, shouting as he comes. Cyrano parries simple and circular, envelopes the blade and carries it round once, twice, and follows the retreating Vicomte with a jump, lunge attack, and thrusting home. The Vicomte falls, coughing. Cyrano recovers, stands upright and salutes.

"A la fin de L'envoi, Je touche."
During the fight the spectators make loud comments, and shout encouragement; and at the end there is loud applause, and congratulations for Cyrano, as the Vicomte's friends carry him off.

CYRANO: Attention! I choose my rhyme. . . . Ah! Here I go.

> With grace I cast my hat away,
> Slowly my great cloak I let fall;
> And forth I shine in grand array,
> Upon my trusty sword, I call.
> It shines as bright as Celadon.
> My feet move fast as Scaramouche.
> Your fate is sealed dear Myrmidon,
> For at the envoi's end I touch.
>
> Take back your gibe, your life to save.
> Continue to fight, and your bird I'll cook.
> I threaten your flank, you smell the grave,
> Defend your heart; to your ribbons look.

My point comes buzzing like a fly,
The coquilles ring like bells in church.
You must decide to live or die,
For at the envoi's end, I touch.

Parry, riposte—I search for a rhyme,
You break, you cower as white as whey.
You wretched man attone your crime.
Tac—and I parry your last essay,
Disarm and I take your weapon away.
I cast it back, you weep too much,
Take your knitting needle and fight and pray.
At the end of the envoi, I will touch.

Envoi

Prince demand of God pardon,
To ask for life would be too much,
Coupe—Beat—Eh Lah! You're gone,
At the envoi's end—I touch.

CHAPTER IX

SMALL SWORD

Comedy Fight, from 'Twelfth Night'

IN the comedy fight between Viola and Sir Andrew Aguecheek, where both unwilling fighters are scared to death of each other, I introduced an old-fashioned type of opening to a fencing match, known as *The Grand Salute*.

This was a sort of limbering-up exercise used by both fencers in exhibition matches. The senior fencer comes on guard and, extending his arm, reverses his blade with the point back over his shoulder, first on the outside line, and then on the inside line, and lunges in sixte, quarte, tierce, and quinte. The opposing fencer shows the parries in these areas and reverses his hand into pronation for the last two. The idea in *Twelfth Night* was to make Sir Andrew do this as a delaying action. There is, of course, no period justification for doing this but it was accepted and got the laughs.

Sir Andrew and Viola are forced forward by Sir Toby and Fabian, their swords scrape together, and they both shrink from the clash of steel. Sir Andrew steps back and goes through the grand salute, while Viola watches. They are then pushed forward again and Sir Andrew does a beat and counter-beat three times on Viola's extended sword. He looks very pleased with himself and attacks with some vigour, with a feint to sixte and a lunge to quarte; Viola parries and retreats. Sir Andrew follows and does his beat and counter-beat again, Viola closes her eyes and extends her arm, Sir Andrew attempts to parry but his sword is carried back by Viola's rush, the hilts come together and both finish up under Sir Andrew's

Fig. 14a

Fig. 14b

Fig. 14. Small Sword.
(a) Black, high attack in Quarte (Number 4); White, parry in Prime (Number 1).
(b) Black, high attack in Sixte (Number 6); White, parry in Seconde (Number 2).

Fig. 14c

Fig. 14d

(c) Black, low attack in Seconde (Number 2); White, parry in Seconde (Number 2).

(d) White attacking at the head on the outside (Sixte Number 6) using the Pass., left foot across the right leading foot. Popular before the lunge.

Fig. 14e

Fig. 14f

(e) Black, a long lunge in high Quarte (Number 4) parried by White in Quarte.
(f) A running attack by White (Fleche) parried by Black in Quarte.

chin, lifting him up on to his toes. This is held a moment, they break, and Antonio rushes forward to the rescue.

The Small Sword or Hanger

The small sword was a great improvement on previous weapons; it was exclusively a thrusting weapon, and was entirely lethal. It was used both for attack and defence, the blade was about thirty-three inches long, and the hand protection consisted of a metal double shell and a knuckle-bow. It was an essential feature of the dress of a gentleman of the eighteenth century. The salute before a bout is like a little dance, and would make a useful contribution to the stage fight.

The Disarm

Disarms, no longer valid in modern fencing, were taught by most of the old masters, and were a feature of sword play until late into the eighteenth century. Seizure of the opponent or his sword with a gloved hand, and following this up with a forward or backward throw, is a method of attack advocated from the early days of the sword. Daggers often had serrated blades so that they could be used to catch a sword and wrest it from the grip of an opponent.

A controlled disarm can be used with good effect in many stage fights, for instance in *The Beaux' Stratagem* small sword fight. Aimwell takes on the two rogues, Hounslow and Bagshot. If he disarmed one of them in an early stage of the fight this would give him a little time to deal with the second highwayman before the first recovered his weapon and came again. A disarm, too, is often a feature of pantomime fights, with the Principal Boy getting the upper hand by this means. In *Hamlet*, a good clean disarm to bring about the exchange of foils is much more satisfactory than messy wrestling, standing on the blade and so on.

G*

The most effective disarm is brought about by engaging in the line of quarte, dominating the opposing blade by bearing down upon it, then making a half-circle underneath and jerking upward. The amount of pressure decides the height the sword will rise when jerked out of the opponent's hand. A heavy parry in seconde will result in a disarm sideways.

Fig. 15a

Fig. 15. The Salute
(a) On guard and take the hat in the left hand.

Safer methods involve the use of the left hand, such as following a parry in tierce, by stepping forward and taking hold of the opponent's sword hand with your left hand; then pushing the arm and sword over to the left, and threatening with your own sword held high. Another method is to parry prime on your opponent's lunge, then move in and slip your left arm over his extended sword and bring the wrist and hand round to catch his wrist; finally bring up the point of your sword and threaten. Again, one can lever down an attacking sword, turning the point downwards and inwards towards the opponent, then reach out the left hand and grip his cross bar, pommel, or the top of the blade, and by

[continued on p. 100

Fig. 15b   Fig. 15c

(b) Swing off the hat with a downward sweep and raise and point the sword. Step forward with the left foot.
(c) Salute with the sword.

Fig. 15d   Fig. 15e

(d) Replace the hat, step forward on guard.
(e) Step forward with the left foot, and salute with the sword again.

Thrust and Parry in Seconde

Quarte

Quarte and Circle Parry

Flacon nade

Fig. 16. Fencing Positions (*Labat*).

Prime

Tierce

Low
Tierce

Seconde

Fig. 17. Fencing Positions (*Danet*).

Half Circle

Octave

Carte

Hand Parry

Fig. 17. Fencing Positions (*Danet*).

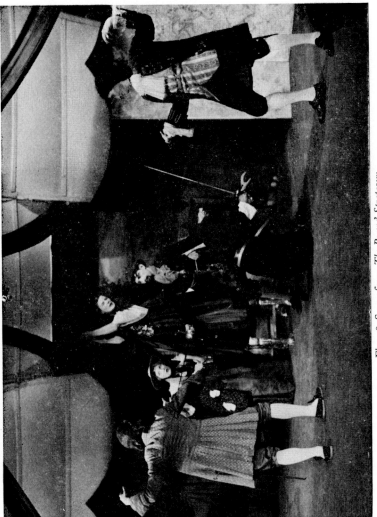

Fig. 18. Scene from *The Beaux' Stratagem.*

Fig. 19a

Fig. 19b

Fig. 19. The Disarm.
(a) Disarm following Parry of Quarte (Position 1).
(b) Disarm after Parry of Quarte (Position 2).

Fig. 19c

Fig. 19d

(c) Disarm after Parry Seconde.
(d) Disarm Final (Position 2).

Fig. 19e

Fig. 19f

(e) Disarm after a Parry on the outside of the sword.
(f) Disarm on Parry Tierce.

Fig. 19g

Fig. 19h

(g) Disarm after Parry Tierce.
(h) Seizure and forward Throw.

Fig. 19i
(i) Seizure and backward Throw.

Fig. 20a

Fig. 20.
(a) "The three-feet" a stop hit by throwing out the left leg behind, and dropping on to the left hand.

Fig. 20b

Fig. 20c

(b) A disarm by White, by bearing down on Black's sword and seizing the hilt with the left hand.
(c) A disarm by White parrying Seconde, winding the left arm round Black's blade and lifting it out of his right hand.

pushing inwards with the sword and pulling outwards with the left hand take the weapon.

Finally one can disarm by a strong lifted septime, as in a parry of quarte to septime, then a sudden sharp lift. The rise of the disarmed weapon can be controlled, and with a lot of practice the sword may be caught in the left hand, as it falls, by a disarmer with dexterity.

CHAPTER X

PROTECTION AND WEARING
OF CUT AND THRUST WEAPONS

TWO-HANDED swords were carried over the shoulder, or by a page or servant, but cut and thrust weapons were usually protected by a scabbard, fitted at the opening and the point with metal. In the case of expensive weapons, the scabbard was often covered with ornamental leather. In the eighteenth century the sword and scabbard were artistically decorated and had special fittings such as a catch to prevent the blade falling out when riding.

Usually the weapon hung from the left hip, either straight from the belt, like the sword of a knight, or suspended from two long hanging straps or a broad sling. The rapier was usually carried in a sling. Small swords and sabres used the two straps. Bandoliers were also used in the seventeenth century, and early eighteenth. These were slung from the right shoulder to the left hip.

CHAPTER XI

BOWIE KNIFE

THE Bowie Knife is worth consideration, for Cowboys and Indians have always been a favourite subject for children's play, and recently there have been a number of successful plays about Indian lore, and most children watch the "Goodies" and "Baddies" in the West on the television screen. It is a type of dagger knife invented by Colonel James Bowie in 1836; it was used as a weapon in the south and south-west of the United States of America. Colonel Bowie and Colonel Davie Crockett died in the massacre of the Alamo—as Walt Whitman puts it:

> "They were the glory of a race of rangers,
> Matchless with a horse, a rifle, a song, a supper or a
> courtship,
> Large, turbulent, brave, handsome, generous, proud
> and affectionate,
> Bearded, sunburnt, dressed in the free costume of
> hunters."

The Bowie knife was the weapon of the mountain men, the frontiersmen, the buffalo hunters, and probably the scalp hunters.

The handle is polished wood fitted to a steel tang, and fastened with two brass rivets. There are four indentations in the handle to give a better grip, and three on the left side of the blade. There is a short cross-bar, and the blade is broad, curving to a fine double-edged point. It can be used for stabbing, slicing or chopping, and makes an excellent throwing knife as the blade is well balanced. Duels were fought with it and in hand-to-hand fighting it was an excellent weapon.

Copies can be moulded in metal, or blunt copies cut from soft steel, with wooden handles attached; and rubber versions are available on the market which look dan-

Fig. 21. The Bowie Knife.

gerous and are particularly safe. Handling a weapon that looks and feels right, can do a great deal to stimulate the imagination of the playing child.

CHAPTER XII

FIGHT ARRANGING NOTES

1. The fight arranger must know the play thoroughly and the players must fight in character.
2. The fight must be orchestrated and the idea that a mistake may mean death should be emphasised in the movement.
3. The amount of space available on stage and the proximity of scenery and properties must be kept in mind in arranging the fights.
4. The pattern of movement must have variety and climaxes must be built.
5. Vocal accompaniment is often a dramatic asset and the surprise element (especially in familiar plays) is essential.
6. Safety precautions must have priority: non-slip shoes and sword handles, safe weapons, a good light, an uncluttered stage and a slow rehearsal progress all make sense.
7. A well rehearsed sequence of attacks and parries must be built up slowly and a slow fight can often be made dramatic. Adequate time must be allowed for rehearsal.
8. Comedy fights must also be worked out and made dramatic.
9. Battles should be approached on the principle of dance drama and the maximum use made of levels.
10. Fights to music and non-realistic and stylised fights are often dramatically effective.
11. Consideration must be given to period and a weapon allied to the costume worn.
12. Fights for schoolchildren should be simple and well rehearsed and cutting sequences are usually much safer than point attacks.

CHAPTER XIII

COSTUMES AND ACCESSORIES

MANY schools and youth clubs are unwilling to attempt costume productions because of the difficulty and expense of hiring suitable garments. The answer to the problem is an adaptable wardrobe, as outlined in a number of costume books, such as Norah Lambourne's *Dressing the Play*. This works on the assumption that all members of the audience have an instinctive feeling about period and are satisfied if the correct silhouette is produced.

An adaptable wardrobe consists of pieces of material, squares and semi-circles, which can be used as cloaks or skirts and need not be cut. Period accessories like shaped sleeves and hoods can also be evolved from these adaptable peces and a wide variety of materials, such as plastic bottles, bottle tops, pan scrubbers and practically anything which would take paint effectively can be adapted for use. A basic costume of tights and close-fitting jersey of a neutral colour enables the costume to be built up. For instance, Elizabethan costume can be created by using a beret cap with a feather, a ruff made of a pie frill, a jerkin which can be adapted from a simple basic shape with puffed sleeves and slashes, or ornamentation fixed on to the basic garment by poppets and the padded breeches or trunks can be filled out with material and again slashed and belted. It is possible to use this adaptable wardrobe with these basic cloak/skirt shapes in plays up to the late seventeenth and eighteenth century where men's coats have to have the tailored look. Here again, a little ingenuity with old modern garments (the maxi skirt would be a godsend) will produce the correct outline.

When people became clothes conscious in the fifteenth/ sixteenth century, the prevailing fashion had an effect on

Fig. 22. *Romeo and Juliet*.
Scene at a School Leaver's Course at Grendon Hall Youth Centre.

the type of weapon and this is particularly noticeable when the square-cut, heavy, thick garments of the Elizabethan and Jacobean period gave place to the silks and satins of the Cavalier period. You have a transformation from the heavy rapier and dagger to the meticulous smaller sword. As far as the early warriors are concerned, the size and length of their weapons largely dictated their deployment of soldiers—the Egyptians and the Greeks who were chariot men or horsemen using a long-bladed weapon; the Roman Cohorts with their spears and their stabbing weapons; the Vikings and Norsemen with their screaming, slashing attacks using round shields and long-bladed weapons again and, of course, spears and axes; the armoured knights who were concerned with breaking plate armour or biting into chainmail, again using heavy and sometimes two-handed weapons. The influence of the various countries which dominated, too, had an effect on weapons—Spain with the long rapier and later France with the small sword. The reaction of the Englishmen who had a sturdy dislike of point work and continued to use cutting weapons is interesting and George Silver wrote a book to prove that a cut was quicker than a stab and challenged the foreign masters to fight with himself and his brother when England was invaded by the Spanish and the French. Shakespeare in *Henry V* and particularly in *Romeo and Juliet* in the Mercutio description of Tybalt brings this out. The popularity in England of the broad sword and back sword lasted into the nineteenth century. The type of fencing which was simple, safe and monotonous called for an eye for distance, judgement of time and a strong forearm and fingers. It is interesting to note that the sword as a weapon of defence as well as offence was not developed until after the invention of gunpowder and that the two-handed sword was used late in the history by Irish mercenaries and Scottish heroes like Alisdair Macdonald, "Col. Kitto", ally of the Great Montrose. The Great Fencing Schools began teaching the science of the sword when armour was discarded. The first experts were from the middle classes and although Edward I made it a law that all Englishmen must be prepared to defend themselves, he also issued an edict against the teaching of fencing. It was not until Henry VIII that fencers became acceptable and this may have some bearing on the close relationship between the fencing masters and the Elizabethan actors. The fencing masters also had a considerable influence on the stage fights mounted by Garrick and his contemporaries and the great Angelo has left an interesting record of his methods. It is also interesting that in the nineteenth century most of the great players were fencers.

After the Restoration the sword became an article of dress and at this date the court sword and military sword part company. Fencing became a courtly accomplishment and much of the basis of modern fencing was brought in at this period. Fencing with the small sword was as polished as Addison and Pope, so that the important thing to remember in period production is that people of that particular period did not know that they were seventeenth- or eighteenth-century men and it is essential that actors do not give the impression that they are people in fancy dress. Even to wear a sword and sit down with it by your side calls for considerable practice and, in order to make the stage fight acceptable and realistic, time must be given to the necessary business of building up cadence and working to a climax and making it a real dramatic experience.

CHAPTER XIV

TYPES OF WEAPON AND METHODS OF MAKING THEM IN SCHOOL HANDICRAFT WORKSHOPS

THE simple method of making a period weapon, either a rapier or a small sword, is to use a modern épée blade for the rapier and a foil blade for the small sword. The old type of foil with the figure of eight guard makes a better weapon, as it has a large metal button and the figure of eight can be filled in and used as a base for the period hilt.

The method of making the rapier is to remove the pommel, grip and coquille or bell guard and make a period type guard, with a cross-bar, welded on, then make and fit a knuckle bow, or basket, suitable to the particular period. Usually it is necessary to build up the grip, either with copper wire or leather, then refit the pommel nut.

With the foil fit a knuckle bow above the coquille, replace the grip and screw on the pommel and you have a passable weapon. The bow is easy to make using either metal or wire.

Most school metal-work shops have cutting, buffing and riveting machines, and if a more difficult type of sword is the object, choose a suitable piece of soft metal (steel), and cut the blade to the shape you require, buff down the edges, and file off smoothly. Brace the blade on both sides by riveting on in the centre a thinner piece of steel, and extending this above the blade to make a tang. Slot in the cross-guard, on each side of the tang,

[continued on p. 116

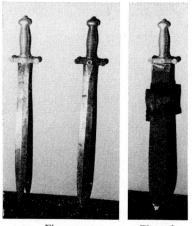

Fig. 23a   Fig. 23b

Fig. 23. Roman type Swords.
(a) Two swords made in the workshop of Roade Secondary School Northamptonshire. Blades of soft steel, and hilts moulded in brass and aluminium.
(b) Sword in a sheath of wooden slats braced with metal. The frog is of leather. Made in the Boot and Shoe College, Rushden.

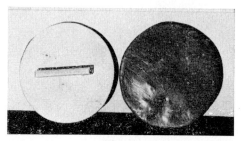

Fig. 24

Fig. 24. Hand Buckler of oak wood with hand grasp, and covered with leather on the outside. Made in the Boot and Shoe College, Rushden.

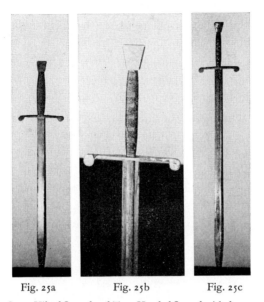

Fig. 25a   Fig. 25b   Fig. 25c

Fig. 25. Cross-Hilted Sword and Two-Handed Sword with decorated Grip

(a) Cross-hilted sword, the blade of soft steel, cross bar and pommel of soft steel, and a fitted handle of soft wood. Made in the workshop of the Roade Secondary School, Northants.

(b) and (c) Two-handed sword with decorated grip, worked pommel and cross-bar, and spliced binding with metal clips on the handles. Blade of soft steel with an extra steel brace spliced on for firmness. Made in the workshop of Corby Beanfield Secondary School, Northamptonshire.

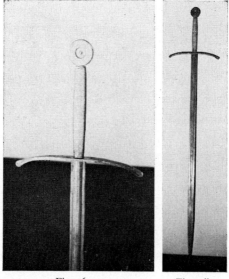

Fig. 26a   Fig. 26b

Fig. 26. Two-Handed Sword.
(a) Decorated hilt with Saxon pattern pommel and copper wire handle.
(b) Sword and hilt tang of soft steel and an extra brace of soft steel spliced on to the blade. Made in the workshop of Corby Beanfield Secondary School.

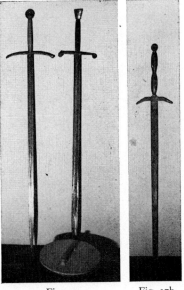

Fig. 27a   Fig. 27b

Fig. 27. Two-Handed Swords.
(a) Two-handed swords made in Corby Beanfield Secondary School and the Moulton Secondary School, Northamptonshire.
(b) A carved handle of oak to give a better grip.

Fig. 28. Period Rapier using a modern épée blade, fitted to a metal Rapier cup, fretted with holes for lightness; a metal cross-bar and knuckle bow added and the handle bound with leather.

Fig. 29a   Fig. 29b

Fig. 29. Rapiers and Dagger.
(a) Period Rapier. A triangular épée blade, made of forged steel and with a button at the tip, makes a very good stage weapon, and can be adapted to cover a wide period by altering the handle to fit the current fashion.
(b) A rapier and dagger, seventeenth century. The dagger made of soft steel with a button at the tip. The handle of plastic riveted on.
All made at the Moulton Secondary School.

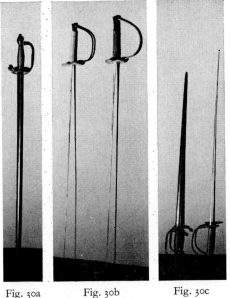

Fig. 30a   Fig. 30b   Fig. 30c

Fig. 30. Small Swords.
(a) An eighteenth century small sword with a brass cup and a brass wire hilt.
(b) Small swords made by fitting metal cups and metal knuckle bows to Figure of Eight foil blades.
(c) Small swords: one of soft steel fitted with a metal hilt and the handle bound with copper wire; the other with a metal hilt fitted to a modern foil blade.
Made at the Weavers Comprehensive School, Wellingborough, Northamptonshire.

and slot in a shaped pommel at the end of the tang. Then bind the grip round the tang using copper wire. The grip can also be made of wood riveted on to the metal of the tang; and metals like aluminium can be moulded to make handles and grips of interesting shapes. The riveted brace on the blade is well worth the extra trouble and can help in the balance of the weapon. The swords will chip after a few fights but a vice and a large file soon puts this right.

LIST OF SUPPLIERS

Swords of York Ltd., 37 Aldwark, York.

Leon Paul Ltd. (Fencing Equipment and Presentation Swords), 39 Neal Street, London, W.C.2.

The Armoury, 36 Earls Court Road, London, W.8.

Robert White & Sons, 57–59 Neal Street, London, W.C.2.

Leichner Ltd. (Make-up and Stage Blood), 436 Essex Road, London, W.1.

SOME AMERICAN SUPPLIERS:

Robert Abel, Inc. (armour and weapons), 157 East 67th Street, New York, N.Y. 10021

Castello Fencing Equipment Co. Inc., 30 East 10th Street, New York, N.Y. 10011

Eaves Costume Co. Inc. (armour, swords and daggers), 151 West 46th Street, New York, N.Y. 10036

Excalibur, Ltd. (manufactures armour and swords), 265 East Main, Centerport, Long Island, New York.

George Santelli, Inc. (fencing equipment) 412 Sixth Avenue, New York, N.Y. 10011.

BIBLIOGRAPHY

AYLWARD, J. D., *The Small Sword in England* (Hutchinson, London, 1945; Fernhill House, Ltd., N.Y.C.).

AYLWARD, J. D. *The House of Angelo* (Batchworth Press, London, 1953).

AYLWARD, J. D. *The English Master of Arms* (Routledge and Kegan Paul, London, 1956).

BALDICK, ROBERT, *The Duel* (Chapman and Hall, London, 1965).

BLACKMORE, HOWARD L., *Arms and Armour* (Studio Vista, London, 1965; E. P. Dutton & Co., N.Y.C.).

CASTLE, EGERTON. *Schools and Masters of Fence* (George Bell, London, 1885; George Shumway, R.D. 7, York, Pennsylvania).

CHOREOLOGY, *Benesh Movement Notation* (Max Parrish, London. Also obtainable from The Institute of Choreology, 4 Margravine Gardens, London, W.6.).

CROSNIER, ROGER, *Fencing with the Foil* (Faber and Faber, London, 1951; A. S. Barnes & Co., Cranbury, New Jersey).

CROSNIER, ROGER, *Fencing with the Sabre*, (Faber and Faber, London, 1954).

CROSNIER, ROGER, *Fencing with the Épée*, (Faber and Faber, London, 1958).

FFOULKES, CHARLES J., *The Armouries of the Tower of London*. Vols. I and II, Her Majesty's Stationery Office, London, 1916).

FORESTIER, AMEDEE, *The Roman Soldier* (A. & C. Black, London, 1928).

HAYWARD, J. F., *Swords and Daggers* (Her Majesty's Stationery Office, London, 1951).

HOBBS, WILLIAM, *The Technique of Stage Fight* (Studio Vista, London, 1967) or *Stage Fight* (American title) (Theatre Arts Books, New York, 1967).

HUTTON, CAPTAIN ALFRED, *Cold Steel* (Clowes, London, 1889).

KENTON, WARREN, *Stage Properties and How to Make Them* (Pitman's Theatre and Stage Series, London, 1964).

LABAN, RUDOLF, *Principles of Dance and Movement Notation* (Macdonald and Evans, London, 1956).

LIDSTONE, R. A., *An Introduction to Kendo* (Judo Ltd., Croydon, Surrey, 1964; Wehman Bros., Hackensack, N.J.).

OAKESHOTT, R. EWART, *The Sword in the Age of Chivalry* (Lutterworth, London, 1964).

POLLOCK, W. H., GROVE, F. C., MITCHELL, E. B., and ARMSTRONG, W., *Fencing, Boxing and Wrestling* (The Badminton Library, Longmans, Green, London, 1890).

SILVER, G., *Paradoxes of Defence* (Shakespeare Association Facsimiles No. 6, Oxford University Press, London, 1933).

SPRAGUE, D. C. *Shakespeare and the Actors* (Harvard University Press).

THOMAS, BRUNO *et al.*, *Arms and Armour* (Thames and Hudson, London, 1964; McGraw-Hill Book Co., N.Y.C.).

TREECE, HENRY and OAKESHOTT, EWART, *Fighting Men* (Brockhampton Press, Leicester, 1963; G. P. Putnam's Sons, N.Y.C.).

WAGNER EDWARD, *Cut and Thrust Weapons* (Spring Books, Drury House, Russell Street, London, W.C.2., 1967; Tudor Publishing Co., N.Y.C.).

WILKINSON, FREDERICK, *Swords and Daggers* (Ward, Lock, London, 1967; Hawthorn Books, Inc., N.Y.C.).

"On Fencing with the Two Handed Sword" in *Reliquiae Antiquae*, Vol. I, (Pickering, 1841). [A copy exists in the library of the University of Nottingham.]

'Rapier and Dagger' in *A New Book of Sports*, reprinted from *The Saturday Review* (Richard Bentley and Son, London, 1885).